SEMINAR STUDIES IN HISTORY

Editor: Patrick Richardson

The Textile Revolution

John Addy

LONGMAN

LONGMAN GROUP LIMITED
London

Associated companies branches and
representatives throughout the world

First published 1976

ISBN 0 582 35220.7

Printed in Great Britain by
Whitstable Litho Ltd, Whitstable, Kent.

Contents

Introduction to the Series

The seminar method of teaching is being used increasingly. It is a way of learning in smaller groups through discussion, designed both to get away from and to supplement the basic lecture techniques. To be successful, the members of a seminar must be informed — or else, in the unkind phrase of a cynic — it can be a 'pooling of ignorance'. The chapter in the textbook of English or European history by its nature cannot provide material in this depth, but at the same time the full academic work may be too long and perhaps too advanced.

For this reason we have invited practising teachers to contribute short studies on specialised aspects of British and European history with these special needs in mind. For this series the authors have been asked to provide, in addition to their basic analysis, a full selection of documentary material of all kinds and an up-to-date and comprehensive bibliography. Both these sections are referred to in the text, but it is hoped that they will prove to be valuable teaching and learning aids in themselves.

Notes on the System of References:
A bold number in round brackets (5) in the text refers the reader to the corresponding entry in the Bibliography section at the end of the book.

A bold number in square brackets, preceded by 'doc' [doc 6, 8] refers the reader to the corresponding items in the section of Documents, which follows the main text.

PATRICK RICHARDSON
General Editor

Foreword

The textile industry is an ancient one with its roots in the twelfth century and not, as many have supposed, based on the domestic system of the early eighteenth century. The wool textile trade had no typical domestic system for there were many varieties of this which depended on a particular geographical area, either Lancashire or Yorkshire, Nottingham or the West of England, East Anglia or the Scottish Border, where textile goods were manufactured. In addition, climate, water supply and its chemical composition, plus inherited skills, all played a part in the development of this industry.

The aim of this study is to trace the evolution of the textile trade from its medieval origins to the expansion of the eighteenth and nineteenth centuries, which resulted from an increase in population and the expansion of overseas markets. The evolution of the mill and the factory system brought great changes to the structure of village and town. As always at a time of industrial change there are people who suffer, so some attention has been given to wages, prices and the impact of external affairs. Illustrations have been included showing how the clothier often became the mill-owner of the nineteenth century.

Since works on textile trades tend to be based on processes rather than on the industry as a whole there is much division and subdivision, this is reflected in the length of the bibliography. The documents have been selected from as many unpublished sources as possible. Some were discovered in private family collections, others in local government archives, but overall the aim is to present a balanced picture, in so far as this can be done, of the industry as a whole. It is hoped that the keen student will find encouragement in this study to delve deeper into the collections of industrial archives in the county record offices. Perhaps it is not too much to hope that some enterprising reader may be stimulated to undertake further research into this fascinating subject for the benefit of future generations.

JOHN ADDY

Acknowledgements

We are grateful to the following for permission to reproduce copyright material:

Borthwick Institute of Historical Research for documents from *Proctor's Trade Papers*; Cheshire County Council Record Office for documents from *Articles Preparatory to Visitation* EDV7/1/83; a document concerning Water Rights at Strines Mill by John Sutcliffe from *Sutcliffe Paper* 133; Lancashire County Council Record Office for documents from Kirkham Parish Records PR827/168, Bishops' Register Transcripts, Scarisbrick Papers DDSc.12/135,Thomas Marsden's Festing Accounts Lancashire Wills, Eccleston Papers DDSc.13, Lancashire Evening Post 1777DP, Quarter Sessions Orders, 1779, 1780, 1781, 1784, Quarter Sessions Petitions 1813, Horrocks of Farnworth D.P.412/58, 83 and the diary of John Ward; Leeds City Libraries for documents from *Earl of Dartmouth Rentals* and *Kirkgate Wills* 1684 DB147/1; Manchester University Press for extracts from *The Cotton Trade and Industrial Lancashire 1660-1780* by A.P. Wadsworth and J.I. Mann; the Halifax Antiquarian Society for documents HAS761-4, HAS321 from *Cornelius Ashworth's Diary 1782-1784;* the Royal Commision on Historical Manuscripts for a letter from Ralph Matthews to the Vicar of Leeds 1588 and an extract from the Kenyon Manuscript, reprinted by permission of the Rt. Hon. Lord Kenyon CBE, DL, LLD, FSA;   the Royal Society for the Encouragement of Arts for an extract from 'Invention of John Kay' by H.T. Wood from *Journal of the Society of Arts* Vol. IX; Sheffield City Libraries for documents from the *Spencer Stanhope Muniments* 60586, 60564, 60607, the *Wentworth Woodhouse Muniments* F.45/117, F.46 and the *Arundel Castle Muniments* ACM/D324, all reprinted by permission of His Grace the Duke of Norfolk, EM. CB, CBE, MC; Her Grace Mary Duchess of Roxburghe for documents from the Crewe papers CM969, 970.

PART ONE

The Background

1   The Historical Setting

The production of textiles, especially woollen cloth, has always been a feature of the economic life of society from the time when men began to wear clothes. Wherever sheep have been bred the wool from the fleece has been used to produce cloth of varying qualities and types. The impetus for the production of wool for weaving into cloth followed the arrival of the Cistercian Order in England in 1138. Totally opposed to the settled way of life of the Benedictine monks, who by the twelfth century had become used to ease and comfort, the Cistercians sought the remote uncolonised areas in the north of England and the Welsh valleys. The land surrounding, for example, the new Cistercian foundations of Whalley, Sawley, Rievaulx and Fountains was unsuitable for the production of arable crops for the soil was poor and thin. There was, however, unlimited pasture available on the hill slopes and soon the Yorkshire moors, the Cumberland fells, the Westmorland and Northumberland hills were covered with sheep. In the west country, the Cotswolds were grazed by great flocks of sheep, and abbeys the size of Fountains or Rievaulx were able to maintain flocks of up to 12,000 in number.

The high quality of English wool attracted the attention of the Flemish and Italian merchants who came over to England to buy the annual clip, for English wool was at that time the finest in Europe for quality. The Spanish merino breed was yet in the distant future. These European merchants, financed by the great banking houses of Fugger, Bardi and Frescobaldi bought the entire clip of an abbey, frequently for a year or more in advance and paying spot cash. Hence the Cistercians were able to provide themselves with capital to extend their activities. By the mid-twelfth century the Cistercians are found entering into contracts with local lords to have the right to graze a certain number of sheep on their land, or buying, or acquiring land in order to create a new type of enclosed farm called a grange **(114)** [**doc. 1**]. In addition to the purchase of wool by exporters there arose another class of merchants known as woolmen or broggers, who went round the scattered farms, 'woolgathering' in small parcels which they sold to the exporting merchants. The wool merchants and the broggers met at fixed centres for buying and selling wool. One of these was at

Northleach, in the Cotswolds, and others were at Lavenham and Sudbury in Suffolk. The parish churches of these wool centres illustrate the wealth that accrued to the community through the wool trade (75, 76).

When Edward III started the Hundred Years War with France in 1337, the wool trade was of sufficient importance to be used as a political and diplomatic weapon to put pressure on the Counts of Flanders to abandon their political support of the French by threatening to sever the supply of wool from England which would mean economic disaster for the Flemish weavers. Edward also saw that wool was a suitable staple commodity for the imposition of an export tax in order to raise money to finance the war, so heavy duties up to $33\frac{1}{3}$ per cent, were levied on sacks of wool, for export. In order to make the collection of the duties efficient, Edward designated certain towns to be the centres of the staple market for wool exports. By 1390 the centre had become fixed in Calais and there the staple remained until the town was finally captured by the French in January 1558. The English towns which were named as staple towns for the collection of wool were Winchester, York, Lincoln, London, Newcastle and Bristol (115). When the Italian merchants refused to grant Edward any further loans, he turned to the new Merchant Staplers for assistance and in return granted the company the monopoly on the export of wool. The price of wool rose so high that foreign manufacturers were unable to compete with the English manufacturers of cloth who bought their wool at a considerably reduced rate.

In the Middle Ages there were few towns or villages that did not produce cloth of some kind. With the invention, during the thirteenth century, of the fulling stocks driven by water power for the rapid finishing of woollen cloth, the industry began to move from the towns to areas close to fast flowing streams. By 1337 a native cloth industry had developed, especially in East Anglia, which the king protected and encouraged by inviting skilled Flemish weavers to come and settle in England where conditions were peaceful and favourable to practise their craft. As the manufacture of cloth became more important, the export of raw wool declined steadily so by the fifteenth century the Merchant Adventurers acquired the exclusive right to export cloth. This merchant company set up trading posts in Flanders, Germany and Scandinavia, whereby English cloth was exchanged for Baltic products.

By the mid-sixteenth century, the Merchant Adventurers were sufficiently strong, with the support of the weavers' guilds, to put pressure on the Edwardian government to pass the Weavers' Acts of 1553 and later the Marian Act of 1558 to try to overcome the effects of the slump in the wool trade. Under the terms of these Acts weavers in the old towns were forbidden to possess more than two looms each and in the rural areas only one. Acts did not apply to the north so the relatively new centres of Manchester, Huddersfield, Halifax, Leeds and Bradford received an impetus to develop their woollen trade. The Statute of Artificers 1563 restricted the exercise of the craft to those who had served an apprenticeship of seven years and empowered the Justices of the Peace to forbid all engaged in the craft, who had not served such an apprenticeship, to cease manufacture **(13)**.

The industry benefited in the latter half of the sixteenth century from the immigration of skilled weavers of fine cloth who fled from the persecutions of the Duke of Alva in the Netherlands, and in the following century by Huguenot refugees from France. By the end of the seventeenth century there were four important areas for the manufacture of cloth in England. The west of England, based on Somerset and Gloucester, produced fine broadcloth and flannel; East Anglia became the home of fine worsteds, while the West Riding, which extended into the Saddleworth and Rochdale districts across the Pennines, became the centre for the manufacture of cheap woollen cloth. In the north-west the weaving centre was in the Kendal area which produced the famous Kendal green cloth. From this association of the industry with the rural area arose the domestic system of manufacture **(141)**.

2 The Domestic System

This system of industry was by no means uniform so far as the production of cloth was concerned. In the west of England, the clothier supervised the manufacture at every stage of production. He organised the industry, supplied the raw wool to the spinners and yarn to the weavers, finally marketing the cloth. Both spinners and weavers often worked for more than one clothier but in this region the apprenticeship system had disappeared by 1700 as a compulsory practice. The clothier sold his product to an exporting merchant in Bakewell Hall, London, or to a travelling chapman from the provinces.

At a very early period the East Anglian trade was divided into two branches, woollen in Suffolk and worsted in Norfolk. This latter county lacked a plentiful supply of water so it had to specialise in a type of cloth that did not require fulling as part of the finishing process. The long strands of wool (four inches and upwards) were used to manufacture a fine cloth which took its name from the village of Worstead in the same county. When Flemish immigrants came into the area they developed the manufacture of a light fabric known as 'new draperies', which became popular in the latter half of the sixteenth century. On the other hand, Suffolk had a plentiful supply of water so the short strands of wool could be used to manufacture a type of woollen cloth known as kersey, which took its name from a village where it was woven. As in the west of England, the East Anglian cloth industry was organised by the wealthy clothiers who bought the Lincoln and Leicester long wool, distributed it to the spinners to convert into yarn and then to the weavers who wove it into cloth.

In the West Riding, the industry developed along different lines. Here the clothier tended to be a small independent man who also farmed in his spare time. He sold his finished cloth in the local market and used the money he received to purchase raw materials for the next piece. Occasionally he employed assistants and owned three or more looms but at first this was exceptional. By 1294 there was already the nucleus of a textile trade in the Huddersfield area when Henry de Lacy, Earl of Lincoln, lord of the honours of Pontefract and Clitheroe. obtained a charter from Edward I empowering him to hold weekly markets at Almondbury (Huddersfield) Pontefract, Bradford and Burnley where there were erected some of the new water driven fulling mills. The adaptation of water power to drive pairs of fulling stocks, in use by the mid-thirteenth century, made the finishing of woollen cloth easier and cheaper. The swift streams of the Pennines, which served both Lancashire and Yorkshire, were utilised by constructing dams to provide a constant supply of water to the fulling mills which were usually erected in the valley bottom below the dam. The fulling mills were occasionally found attached to a corn mill already established. The Lay Subsidy Rolls (16) give evidence of the existence of the fuller's craft through the use of surnames such as John the Tynctor, Ralph the Fuller, and John the Walker. Other evidence exists concerning the woollen industry in the court rolls of the manor of Wakefield which covered most of the Calder valley (17).

By the seventeenth century, the northern textile industry was expanding. The kersey was by now well known throughout western Europe, and some attempt had been made to standardise the length and width of the pieces. In 1552 it was determined that the length of the kersey should be seventeen or eighteen yards in length weighing about twenty pounds a piece in the finished state. Leeds clothiers were beginning to weave broadcloth which was twenty-four yards in length and in width, 'two ells between the selvedge'. This type of cloth became known as the 'northern dozens', a cloth which had improved vastly since the thirteenth century when it was said to be full of holes and of poor quality.

The domestic system of cloth manufacture was never so simple a method of production as some would have us believe, nor, as the term implies, was it confined entirely to the dwelling house. In reality it was a most complex system with a number of variations throughout the country and by no means was it the universal practice for the woollen or cotton weaver to be a self-employed person producing his cloth from start to finish and acting as a personal salesman in the market. Admittedly the West Riding clothier was often, but by no means always, a master clothier in his own household. The majority produced only a part of the final product and the houses were often workshops where spinners and weavers were employed by master clothiers. The industry was organised on capitalist lines from the early days since sheep farmers were paid in cash for their wool. Production was coordinated between spinners, carders, weavers and finishers who were often living at some distance apart. Finally there was the sale of the finished pieces to be organised in the cloth market. So there are to be found wool staplers and yarn merchants who employed spinners and

7

marketed the yarn. There were clothiers who bought wool and yarn to weave into cloth on their own looms. Some clothiers were men of wealth and others were wage-earning manual workers. This well established capitalist industry made the transfer to a factory system of production fairly easy when the time came for the change to be made **(1)**.

Large numbers of Yorkshire and Lancashire textile workers lived in stone built cottages but worked in the small loom shops owned by the master clothiers. Others lived in stone cottages with long windows in the upper storeys divided by stone mullions in order to throw light on the looms. Travellers using the trans-Pennine railway route from Leeds to Manchester may observe, as they travel along the Colne Valley to Standedge tunnel and also at Saddleworth on the other side, long rows of weavers' cottages built close to a clothier's warehouse. These cottages often appear to be built on three sides of a rectangle or facing the road and many still survive in a well preserved condition.

Some light is thrown on the process of the manufacture of cloth by Ralph Matthews, who was replying to a letter written to him in 1588 by the vicar of Leeds concerning the quantity of wool required to keep sixty persons fully employed [doc. 2]. Matthews also commented on the qualities of wool that was intended to be used. It would appear from his calculations that one spinner could produce about seven pounds of woollen yarn in one week and that ten pieces could be woven by eight weavers each week for the market. Another feature is the ability to purchase wool from a wider area than previously, due to slightly better communications.

Daniel Defoe **(2)** was impressed by the busy industrious life of Halifax, pointing out the prosperity of the clothiers and their employees. He gives no indication of the complexity of the processes involved and of the risks that attended those who embarked on the practice of cloth manufacture [doc. 3]. The first stage in the process was to scour the wool and remove by hand-picking all the foreign matter, a process which on occasions was followed by dyeing the raw wool in a lead or dye house. Afterwards the scoured wool was oiled, to make the carding process easier, butter acting as a substitute if foreign oils were unobtainable. It was the recognised custom to use homemade products until the chemical dyestuffs became available in the later nineteenth century. A pair of hand cards, looking like wire brushes in which hooked iron staples were inserted, were used to card the wool and straighten out the fibres into a sliver for spinning. A weaver or small clothier would have the spinning carried out at home but the larger clothier usually put out the spinning to be undertaken by cottagers from whom he would collect the spun yarn. Thomas Marsden of Bolton practised this method and he named his yarns from the villages in which the spinning was undertaken [doc. 4]. The Lancashire spinning wheel was a large, single thread wheel known as a 'jersey wheel'. It was a rough and ready construction on which, by revolving the wheel in a clockwise direction, the sliver was spun into a single thread. By reversing the direction of the wheel, the spun thread was wound on a bobbin for either weft or warp package (32) [doc. 5]. Sizing and beaming of the warp followed and then the weaving of the piece. The next process was wet and messy for the piece had to be scoured to remove grease. The liquid used was stale urine or 'weeting' as it was locally termed. This remained the standard scouring liquid until the gas works began to produce a cheap quality of ammonia. The stone floor of the living room was often used for scouring the piece. All the furniture, having been removed, the piece was spread over the floor, sprinkled well with urine from a garden watering can and scrubbed. The piece was then rolled up and taken to the fulling mill for thickening by pounding the piece under a pair of heavy fulling stocks in a tank of soapy water. The piece was then dyed if required, a process by no means easy with certain colours [doc. 6] (98).

The gentry saw that there was money to be made by erecting a fulling mill, so alongside the Pennine streams there appeared a series of such mills which were rented out to a miller, who made his own profit from the cloth he fulled. Usually these mills operated in winter and spring to avoid the summer drought but occasionally the combined effects of winter frost and summer drought could be serious as the records of Slaithwaite fulling mills reveal [doc. 7]. The piece was then taken home and stretched on a tenter frame to dry the cloth and prevent shrinking. These tenter frames were outside and the name has survived in such terms as tentercroft, tenter hill close and other similar locations. The final process was to brush the cloth surface with teazels in order to raise the nap and the piece was then sheared or cropped by means of a pair of large hand shears to produce a smooth surface. The finished piece was folded and taken to be sold at one of the local cloth markets in either Huddersfield, Halifax, Leeds, or Manchester (89). Cotton or fustian was manufactured by a very similar process but in this case the finishing process included bleaching of the cloth. Fustian was a product obtained by using a linen warp, made from imported or homegrown flax, and woollen weft. Government restrictions on the manufacture of pure cotton cloth, in order to protect the

Indian muslin industry, made it essential to weave an artificial type of cotton cloth until the restrictions were removed in the mid-eighteenth century **(62)**.

Originally the local cloth markets operated in the open air, on the churchyard wall, or on the bridge over the river Aire at Leeds. The increasing amount of business, which was transacted in the eighteenth century, led to the building of cloth halls. Halifax was the earliest, followed by Leeds, which had two cloth halls in 1755 and one at Wakefield. In 1766, Sir John Ramsden, lord of the manor of Huddersfield, built a cloth hall in the town but less than twenty years later it was necessary to enlarge the building **(61)**. Room was provided for 116 stalls on the ground floor and a further fifty-two in the balcony. However the change in the pattern of trade after 1870 led to the decline of the cloth hall and it was demolished in 1930 to make way for a cinema. The front entrance with the clock is preserved in Ravensknowle Park, Huddersfield. The clothiers in the Penistone area, of whom there appear to have been ninety-one, found by experience that the prospects for a cloth market in Penistone were more favourable than the expensive alternative of carrying the cloth to sell in Sheffield some fifteen miles distant. Encouraged by their success, the clothiers entered into an agreement with three local gentlemen to create a market at Penistone. A cloth hall was erected, which, though sadly mutilated, still stands in the centre of the town. These clothiers were supported in their action by the tenants of the three Thurlstone fulling mills who entered into a bond of forty pounds not to full cloth for those who had not signed the market agreement [**doc. 8**].

During the seventeenth century an export trade existed, of some importance, between York and Hull with the ports of Amsterdam, Bergen, Hamburg, Stockholm, Danzig and inland to Königsberg. Since the proctors in the ecclesiastical courts of the Archbishop of York were also civil lawyers, by some chance their civil papers became mixed with the consistory court papers at the York registry. Hence the survival of these documents make it possible to reconstruct a detailed picture of this export trade in cloth **(116)** [**doc. 9**]. By 1750, Samuel Hill a clothier of Soyland, Halifax, was exporting his cloth to Königsberg and Russia, sending his pattern lists as far afield as Persia via St Petersburg and Astrakhan. Some merchants travelled overseas with their cloth and sometimes failed to return. In February 1573, John Armitage of Farnley Tyas, Huddersfield set sail in the ship *Jesus of Hull* from Liverpool to Carrickfergus with a load of cloth. During the voyage the ship was wrecked and the passengers and crew were all murdered by the Irish kernes **(135)**.

John Oldfield, recording details of life in the village of Netherton, Huddersfield, described the organisation of the woollen trade in 1860 [**doc. 10**]. A typical eighteenth-century clothier's house was a low building, with a warehouse at one end in which to store finished pieces and sometimes a barn, stable, or cow house at the opposite end. How numerous clothiers and weavers were may be noted from the estimates made by W.B. Crump and Miss G. Ghorbal of looms in Saddleworth **(61)**. They have calculated that in the early nineteenth century there were 2,000 looms at work in this village where the finest Yorkshire cloth was woven at this time. An examination of the wills and inventories of clothiers enables a reconstruction to be made of the extent of their business interest and prosperity. The will of Joseph Langfield of Horbury in 1746, shows that he owned his own tenter and dyehouse in addition to his looms. On the other hand the inventory of Joshua Wood of Cumberworth, Huddersfield, dated 7 February 1786 indicates that he sold cloth as far distant as Yarmouth, London, Downham Market and Gretna Green **(20)**.

The Leeds clothiers had no interest in agricultural pursuits as such and were content with a house, parlour (bed room), a small parlour and a workshop with either looms or shears. The outstanding debts as recorded in their inventories show that their business interests were not small [**doc. 11**]. The recently discovered diary of Cornelius Ashworth, a Halifax clothier, illustrates not only the wide variety of a clothier's life but also the problems of transporting and selling cloth [**doc. 12**].

The majority of these clothiers had one or more apprentices bound to them, often under the terms of a charity [**doc. 13**] to be taught to write, prepare accounts and learn the craft over a period of seven years. There were exceptions to this custom, as may be observed from the terms of the apprenticeship of John Roberts of Wooldale to Luke Firth of Holmfirth in 1602. In this case the apprentice was bound for six years to be taught the 'science of cloth working and weaving the broad lombes'. In another case the apprentice was bound for nine years to learn 'the traid of dyeing, warping, weaving, sheering and all other things to the said traid and occupation of cloth-working belonging' **(109)**. A similar pattern of domestic industry existed in Lancashire but, according to Samuel Bamford, the interior arrangement of the weaver's cottage was somewhat different to his Yorkshire counterpart [**doc. 14**]. The smallholding often attached to the manufacturing house was expected to raise the rent, but if it failed to do so then the profits of industry came to the rescue **(32)**.

Ralph Thoresby, writing of the Leeds House of Correction in 1715, remarked that the inmates were taught to scribble, which was then a

11

new invention for mixing the colours of dyed wool to produce a certain blend (60). Morehouse describes this system of scribbling as being the practice at Holmfirth, before 1750, in the manufacture of cloth known as 'Leeds Reds'. He recorded that these goods were manufactured in the old way, the wool being scribbled and carded by hand cards, spun on a single thread wheel and woven by the hand shuttle (109). This new term, 'scribbler' gradually replaced the older term of 'carder' where wool was prepared by the use of hand cards as in the West Riding. On the other hand, Lancashire retained the term 'carder'. This distinction survives at the present time, where in the West Riding, a woollen carder is known as a scribbling engineer and in Lancashire as a card room operative. The evidence for the change in terminology may be noted in the registers of Saddleworth chapel from 1736 onwards, where the occupation of scribbler replaces that of carder. Moving over to Bury and Newchurch the registers there record carders and never scribblers (70).

The entire future of the textile industry and its development lay in the improvement of communications. The pack horse trains, which traversed the Pennines, were subject to weather conditions and in the winter months this traffic virtually ceased [doc. 15]. By 1690 it was clear that there was a need for easier communication between the Lancashire and Yorkshire market towns and the ports on either side of the Pennines. Leeds and Halifax tended to look towards Hull, and Liverpool had an eye on improved communications with London (35).

The first stage in this improved communication system was the construction of the Aire and Calder Navigation to connect Leeds and Wakefield with Goole and Hull. In 1758 the Calder and Hebble Navigation Act enabled the canal to be extended to Sowerby Bridge and so cover the Halifax area (121). The Lancashire canal system was the work of the Duke of Bridgewater and James Brindley, primarily for coal in the early stages, but later for cotton and other goods. The linking of Manchester and Liverpool by canal was an early achievement for by 1740 Manchester was becoming the market centre for cotton goods (83). Not until the nineteenth century was there sufficient engineering skill available to construct a canal across the Pennines by means of a tunnel.

The traditional highways were also improved. In 1732 Manchester constructed the turnpike road through Longendale to the county boundary at Saltersbrook. Three years later the turnpike road from Manchester to Oldham was constructed. A further development took place in 1735 with the turnpike road from Rochdale to Halifax via Blackstone Edge and an extension to Elland. This was followed a few years later by the extension of this turnpike to Leeds **(35)**. It was not until 1759 that the necessary powers were obtained to extend the turnpike from Oldham to Huddersfield via the Standedge route. The Holme valley was opened up by extending the turnpike from Saltersbrook in 1769. Not until 1777 was an attempt made to connect Halifax and Huddersfield with Penistone and Sheffield. At the close of the century, Manchester was connected to the growing cotton towns of Bury, Bolton, Burnley, Blackburn, Preston and Wigan for the better marketing of their products. The demand for cotton goods was expanding, partly as the result of an increase in population and partly from the fact that cotton goods were easier to wash than woollens. There was also a new market opening up for cotton in the American plantations where the fabric was needed to clothe Negro slaves **(31)**. The combined demand exceeded the ability of the domestic production units to satisfy so it was essential to discover some new method by which production could be increased. The result was that a number of Lancashire men with enquiring and scientific minds set about making the essential improvements, with dramatic results in the long term **(70)**.

PART TWO

Analysis

3 The Inventors

In the early stages of development no one had a mill in mind as the ultimate end of the process but merely as a method to speed up domestic production. The first improvement came in the weaving section of the industry. To weave cloth more than thirty-six inches in width required two men to throw the shuttle across the raceboard to one another, a slow cumbersome method of production. It was John Kay of Bolton who first came on the idea of designing some attachment that would enable one weaver to weave cloth of any width without assistance. Kay was the youngest of five children and was born at Walmersley near Bolton in 1704. His father farmed some forty acres of land and in due course apprenticed John to learn the trade of a reed maker. Trained in the craft of making cane reeds, he eventually found that metal reeds led to fewer breakages of the warp thread because the friction between the reed and the thread was considerably reduced. This development aroused no animosity for no one felt that their employment was threatened **(103)**. His next improvement was a new type of shuttle.

In 1733 Kay applied for a patent to protect his new shuttle design, which was described as a wheel or flying shuttle, for the shuttle had wheels fitted underneath to enable it to run easily and smoothly across the raceboard of the loom. The shuttle was propelled across the loom by means of a spring-loaded picking stick. With the aid of this shuttle, one man could weave cloth of any width far quicker than before and so produce more pieces each week. Since the bobbin in the shuttle now revolved more rapidly to release the weft there were many breakages of yarn, hence an improved technique in winding yarn on the bobbin had to be found. This was achieved by winding the yarn on a bobbin in the shape of a cone and fixing the bobbin in the shuttle in a stationary position.

The weavers in Bury, where the new shuttle was introduced, feared the new invention would take away their employment, so there were threats to kill Kay. The attitude of the mob became so violent that he had to flee. The Colchester weavers said Kay would destroy their employment, and the Leeds manufacturers, in 1738, refused to pay any royalties to Kay but were very willing to make use of his shuttle. In subsequent law suits on this matter Kay was ruined by the costs (33). Although he petitioned the government, from time to time, for assistance, there was no response [doc. 6]. Kay went to France where he received some assistance, but despite further applications to the British government for some reward for his invention he received nothing. During the winter of 1780-81 Kay died in poverty. The flying shuttle was a great success and output from the looms increased. However many weavers believed it was in their interest to loiter and waste time so that their employers would not realise the real advantage of the flying shuttle [doc. 17].

Within a few years, the increasing demand for yarn by the weavers led to a shortage in supply so that by 1760 it was taking eight spinners to keep one weaver supplied. Hence the next invention would have to be in the spinning process. The serious shortage of spun yarn encouraged the Society of Arts to offer a prize in 1761 to anyone who could invent a machine which could spin six threads at one time, but no one came forward with any ideas (44).

In 1764 a spinning machine suitable for use in domestic industry was produced by James Hargreaves (29). Hargreaves was born about 1720 in the village of Oswaldtwistle, not far from Accrington. He worked secretly on his design and produced a hand spinning machine, based on the old single thread wheel, which could spin six threads at one time. When Robert Peel discovered that increased amounts of yarn were being produced in the area he made some enquiries and eventually tracked down Hargreaves, and later used some of these machines in his premises at Bury. Hargreaves named his new machine a 'jenny', a corruption of the term 'engine', and this new machine was soon being discussed in the area. Spinners were afraid the new machine would produce so much yarn that their livelihood was in danger, and in 1768, Hargreaves's house was attacked and his furniture destroyed by the mob. He himself had to go into hiding and shortly afterwards made his way to Nottingham where he went into partnership with Thomas James, and together they ran a fairly successful cotton spinning business. Hargreaves neglected to take out a patent for his jenny until 1770 and by this time large numbers had been constructed in Lancashire, where the magistrates encouraged the use of this machine [doc. 18].

The quality of yarn produced on the jenny was unsuitable for use on the stocking frame for hosiery knitting but ideal as weft in the weaving of cotton fabrics. By 1776 the jenny had appeared in the Huddersfield area for spinning wool, being a suitable machine for producing soft woollen yarn (89). The jenny was a cheap machine to manufacture and ideal for use in domestic industry. Indeed the flying shuttle and spinning jenny were found in every clothier's home and spinner's cottage for the next fifty years. Some attempt was made in 1772 by Coniah Wood to improve the jenny, but his invention was never popular. By the end of the century, the jenny had been replaced in Lancashire by Arkwright's water frame and Crompton's mule.

As early as 1740, Lewis Paul and John Wyatt had designed a machine for spinning cotton by means of revolving rollers at varying speeds based on a machine of circular design. Wyatt records that his father, Charles, had produced a machine for making cotton yarn without the assistance of human hands (51). A few of these machines found their way into Halifax but Wyatt made no money from the invention and it was not a practical success (70). It was Arkwright who took over this invention and made it successful. Richard Arkwright was born in Preston in 1732 to a family of thirteen children of poor parents. Having little education, he was trained as a barber and wig maker. Later he removed to Bolton where he set up his own business where he undoubtedly learned about the acute shortage of spun yarn [doc. 19]. The reason for the shortage was not so much the inability of the spinners to cope with demand, but more to the irregularity of the size and degree of twist in the spun cotton yarn. At the time of his second marriage in 1761 to a Miss Biggin of Leigh, Arkwright came into contact with another John Kay, the local clockmaker, who was interested in making mechanical models. Arkwright knew of the existence of Lewis Paul's machine and, with the assistance of Kay, a spinning frame was produced, based on a rectangular design that, in the end, became popular (73). Rumours about this new machine began to circulate in the Preston area and some hostility appeared. To avoid trouble Arkwright moved to Nottingham where he found that the yarn produced on his machine was more suitable for the stocking knitters than that produced on the jenny. He was fortunate to find a partner in Jedediah Strutt, a hosiery manufacturer, and a partnership was formed which in 1771 led to the foundation of a spinning business at Cromford. Here was the necessary water power to drive the new machine. So successful was this first venture that a second mill was erected in Belper. This water frame, although based on the ideas of Lewis Paul, was not a suitable machine for use in domestic industry. It needed water power to drive it, and so the mill emerged as a suitable building to house spinning frames driven by water power. By 1780 there were twenty such mills in Lancashire using Arkwright's water frame under licence. Arkwright was now at the height of his power, travelling frequently between Lancashire, Cheshire and Derbyshire in connection with his business activities. He was knighted in 1786 but only lived a further six years before dying at the age of fifty-nine. The yarn produced by the water frame was a smooth twist resulting from the use of a flyer spinning system. In 1775 the yarn was given a high twist ratio to make it strong enough for cotton warps. This meant that the linen warp could be replaced by one of cotton and so pure cotton goods could be manufactured (**140**).

Before any further improvements could be made in spinning, it was essential to find some means of removing seeds and other impurities from the raw cotton and then to open the fibres. A device, termed a scutching or blowing machine, which incorporated a fan for blowing the raw cotton through and a beater to strike the cotton, assisted better preparation. This machine was first used in Paisley in 1787 and was based on the same principle as the threshing machine. The cotton was beaten with considerable force as it passed over parallel bars, so spaced as to permit the seeds to fall through. Arkwright designed a carding engine for more efficient preparation of cotton prior to spinning but little is known about this.

As the cotton industry expanded it became increasingly essential to reduce handling costs by removing the seeds from, and compressing the raw cotton into bales before shipping. A simple device of a pair of wooden rollers, mounted on a frame and looking very much like an old fashioned mangle or wringing machine and hand operated, was far too slow. In 1794 Eli Witney, who lived in the cotton growing states, designed a gin worked by a horse, and one man was now in a position to undertake the work of fifty men under the old system. This invention speeded up deliveries of raw cotton to feed the new water spinning frames (**70**). The real breakthrough in spinning was made by Samuel Crompton, a native of Bolton. He commenced to spin yarn on a jenny in 1779 to supply the family weavers with cotton weft. At that time the jenny was in the early stages of development so that in all probability it was rather inefficient. Crompton was dissatisfied with the quality of the yarn produced by the jenny and within the next three years he was considering, very seriously, the possibility of improving the method of spinning. In the end he combined the variable speed rollers of the water frame with the movable carriage of the jenny for stretching, spinning, twisting and finally winding the yarn on the bobbins or warp cops using one machine (**100**). No doubt someone thought a combination of this nature should be called a mule and the name stuck [**doc. 20**]. Working secretly at his Bolton home of Hall-i'th-Wood, he successfully produced the fine yarn needed for muslins and strong enough to be used for warps.

The first mule was constructed of wood and carried twenty spindles, being small enough to use in a cottage (74). In 1783 metal rollers were added and the mule enlarged to carry 400 spindles (74). Further improvements were made in 1790 by William Kelly who made the mule semi-automatic and containing a larger number of spindles. The later work of Richard Roberts enabled the mule to become a fully automatic machine between 1825 and 1830. By 1812 there were more than five million spindles at work and the weaving of muslins was now a proven factor for 1,000 looms were engaged in weaving this type of cloth by the end of the century. About 1780 Crompton was persuaded by a number of manufacturers to make the mule public in return for an unspecified sum of money. This payment failed to materialise, for several manufacturers never honoured their agreement. In the end Crompton received about £62 and died a poor man while others made fortunes from his invention. In course of time Bolton became the centre for the spinning of the finest cotton yarn used in the production of high quality fabrics at reasonable prices (65).

The next step was to design a power loom for weaving and so replace the hand loom. W.D. Chapman points out that there was already a narrow fabric loom in existence for weaving ribbon and by 1750 about 1,500 of these Dutch looms, as they were known, were at work in Manchester in special buildings, so marking a halfway stage to the factory (53).

The large output of spun yarn from the new machines provided an impetus to discover new methods of increasing the speed of weaving pieces. In 1774 Robert and Thomas Barber of Bilsborough, Nottingham, designed a loom to be driven by men or horses but they had not the tenacity to pursue it to success. In the end it was the Rev. Edmund Cartwright, rector of Goadly, who produced a clumsy type of loom which could be operated by water power, but which was not a success in the commercial field. Others, like John Austin of Glasgow (1789) and J.L. Robertson of the same city (1795), both tried to produce a commercially viable loom but failed to do so (33). Meanwhile the production of hand looms was increased through the work of Thomas Johnson of Mellor in Cheshire, who designed a take-up motion which automatically wound the cloth on a roller as it was woven. The commercial success of the power loom was due to work of William Horrocks of Stockport who, in 1803, patented a crankshaft motion to drive the sley. Richard Roberts improved on this in 1822 when he replaced many of the wooden parts, including the framework, by parts made of cast iron. Twenty years later the loom was further improved by the addition of a weft stop motion to stop the loom when the weft broke. The addition of a fast reed to protect the warp enabled the loom to be run at double speed. In 1760 John Kay had invented the rising or drop box which, with the circular box in 1854, enabled fancy cloths to be woven without stopping the loom to change shuttles holding different coloured weft (70).

In the woollen and worsted trade, machinery was introduced more slowly due to the use of different raw materials and a long inherited tradition of skill. For centuries wool was combed by hand until Ben Noble invented his combing machine in 1853, to be followed three years later by another designed by Isaac Holden. In the long run the Noble comb proved to be the more popular (97). Also Arkwright's carding machine played a large part in transforming the woollen industry, for, with the addition of a crank and comb motion for doffing the cardings, the process was continuous and automatic. Similar machines to Arkwright's carder were in use in the West Riding before 1780 for scribbling wool. These early machines were very small, hand-operated affairs, though later a horse gin was installed to drive the larger carding machines (52). Later still the machines were transferred to the fulling mill where the water wheel used to drive the fulling stocks also drove the carding machines. H.J. Morehouse (109) writing about Holmfirth, says that the first scribbling machine in that area was installed at Ing Nook Mill about 1780. He describes them as crude machines producing wool in the form of flocks, until the addition of the fly or fancy roller improved it. The issue of the *Leeds Mercury* for January 1779 contains a sale notice giving a detailed description of a scribbling machine; the earliest recorded reference to a carder [doc. 21].

The clothiers appear to have purchased carding machines and either bought or rented an old fulling mill, or built a new one, in which to scribble wool for themselves or their customers. The diary of Joseph Rogerson of Bramley, Leeds (89), describes how the scribbling machines fitted into the domestic system. The Leeds clothiers objected to the introduction of these machines on the grounds that they would throw thousands out of work and limit apprentices to one per unemployed family. A petition was raised in 1786 [doc. 22] against any further machines being introduced into the area, for there were 170 such machines at work within an area seventeen miles south-west of Leeds. The machines were extensively used in Huddersfield and Halifax, but only about forty were driven by horse gin. By 1790 the scribbling machine had assumed the form it was to retain for another generation (61). The scribbling mill performed a double duty for customers.

Carded wool was brought to the mill, by the small manufacturer, who slubbed the cardings and returned them ready for winding on the bobbins. Later the woven cloth was brought back to the mill for scouring and fulling.

There were four machines involved in the scribbling process; the willy or teazer (to open and blend the wool); the scribbling engine proper, the carder which consisted of a number of rollers revolving on a central one called the swift (the rollers being covered with wire cards to straighten the fibres), and lastly the slubbing billy. This latter originated with the jenny and was hand-operated. It demanded great skill to operate it compared with the jenny, so jenny spinning remained a poorly paid cottage craft, while slubbing became a highly paid craft. The object behind slubbing was to draw the loose carding together and give the yarn a twist so that it would be wound on bobbins. The billy had forty spindles mounted on a heavy moving carriage. In operation, about eight inches of the cardings were released and drawn out to seventy inches by pushing the carriage away from the operator and revolving the spindles. The twisted yarn was wound on the bobbins fitted on the spindles. The operator was known as a slubber, assisted by young children called pieceners who joined the new cardings on to the ends of the old by rubbing them together. This gave rise to the employment of very young children to do this job which, under the factory system, gave rise to great abuses (27).

4 The Emergence of the Factory

Apart from one or two abortive attempts to introduce a factory system for the textile industry at the close of the sixteenth century, the first real attempts were made in the first quarter of the eighteenth century. In 1704 Thomas Cotchett of London obtained a lease of rights in the Derwent from the Mayor and Corporation of Derby to erect a silk spinning mill. In 1713 Cotchett became bankrupt and the mill was leased to John and Thomas Lombe for spinning and reeling silk. The mill was successful as the result of order and discipline by the manager and formed the model for six other mills at Stockport, Macclesfield, Congleton, Sheffield and Watford. As Chapman points out (51) these silk mills influenced the design of the Strutt factories at Belper and Cromford. The next to erect a factory was James Hargreaves who came to Nottingham where his building was three storeys high and 130 feet long, for operating the spinning jenny as well as the water-powered carding engines. Richard Arkwright followed and built his mill close to that of Hargreaves. It was at Hargreaves's mill where Arkwright first met his future partner, Jedediah Strutt, who had come to see the water frame in operation. The result of that meeting was a business partnership between Arkwright and Strutt that led to the building of the mills at Cromford (73). Mills had of necessity to be built where a ready supply of water was available and where dams for water storage could be constructed easily, with an arrangement of sluices and shuttles to control the supply of water to the wheel and a tail goit to prevent the used water fouling the wheel by standing at some depth in the mill race. The design of the wheel, either overshot, undershot or breastfall, depended on the situation of the water-supply. In the West Riding, the valleys of the Aire, Calder, Colne and Holme saw the fulling mills expand into scribbling and spinning mills. Ottiwells mill near Marsden, which figures in the Luddite riots, was one of these. The design of the mill was rectangular in form, of one or more storeys, constructed near a powerful stream of water in a narrow part of the valley where a good head or fall of water could be arranged (71).

It was in these remote valleys that the factory system began, away and remote from the industrial centres, often in small hamlets where the supply of labour was a problem and communications frequently difficult (48, 57). These mills required a disciplined and punctual working force, which could appear at a set time to maintain continuous production of cotton yarn. The habits of the native inhabitants of these river valleys had to be changed from those of ignorant, rough men and women who worked when they desired and served no master but themselves. The Arkwrights and Strutts solved the problem by building houses for whole families and so creating the new communities of Belper and Cromford (73). In other areas the community itself was changing as industrial expansion imposed a new structure. In 1778 Beilby Porteus, Bishop of Chester, held his primary visitation. Amongst other matters about which he required information was the size and structure of each parish. In his reply, the vicar of Bolton pointed out that the advent of industry had driven the old settled families to seek new residences in a more amenable area, so leaving Bolton to industrial development [doc. 23], a pattern repeated over and over again in east Lancashire and elsewhere.

The erection of a new mill was no light undertaking, as a study of the plans of Richard Arkwright for his Birkacre mill, Chorley, in 1777 reveals. It was not the mill building itself which was expensive but the machines to equip it. These machines cost Arkwright £900, to which was added the cost of cutting goits for the water supply, building dams, with reinforced banks and finally the water wheel itself [doc. 24]. From a study of the lease granted to Arkwright by John Chadwick it would appear that it was the custom to use, where possible, an old corn mill where water supplies were more or less to hand (137). The terms of the lease appear to be for three lives at a rent of twenty shillings per annum for each foot of waterfall when the mill was in operation, at the same time protecting the interests of the farmers in whose land such water rights were operative (13). At Heptonstall, Halifax, two landowners came to terms concerning the supply of water for a mill. John Foster, owner of Strines estate, and John Entwistle, owner of Ramsden estate, agreed to allow the water which flowed down Ramsden Clough to the top goit of Strines mill to be used for a cotton mill to be erected there, with the construction of a private road to the mill leading from the Halifax and Burnley turnpike [doc. 25].

The plentiful supply of water led to the erection of no less than forty spinning mills in south Lancashire by 1788. Cotton mills were also erected in Yorkshire at Todmorden, Halifax and Keighley, where the eastern slopes of the Pennines provided a plentiful water supply. Mills were also found in Kendal, Ulverston and New Lanark, in Scotland, where David Dale built the mills later taken over by Robert

Owen **(64)**. It was the custom for the factory owner to live in a house close to the mill or even in the mill yard itself. An excellent example of this can be seen at Hartcliffe mills, Denby Dale, Huddersfield, where the original house stands in the mill yard but is now used as offices. Another example can be seen at Queensbury, Bradford, where the house of John Foster, the founder of Black Dyke mills, is preserved and illustrates the conversion of a clothier's house to a mill **(125)**.

It was the steam engine which created the factory of the nineteenth century. Newcomen's engine, developed in the first decade of the eighteenth century, was often used to pump back the water from the tail goit to the mill dam for repeated use, especially when water was in short supply. This engine was costly to run since its consumption of coal was high. It was James Watt **(102)** who turned his attention to the improvement of the Newcomen engine to make it suitable for driving machines. His first improvement was the addition of a separate condenser so that the cylinder remained hot all the time and the necessity to cool it between each stroke of the piston was removed. Until 1774 his experiments were financed by John Roebuck, who became bankrupt and his share in Watt's patent had to be sold. The purchaser was Matthew Boulton of Birmingham who had, at his Soho works, the skilled craftsmen necessary to build the engine; moreover sound iron castings could be obtained from the Coalbrookdale foundries. The cannon boring lathe, designed by John Wilkinson, could be adapted for the accurate boring of the cylinders and so an efficient engine was produced, but nevertheless it could only be used for pumping purposes. R.P. Dobson **(65)** says that Arkwright installed a Boulton and Watt engine in 1780 to pump water from the Derwent for his mills, and that a Bolton mill used the same make of engine to raise water from the dam to the wheel.

The real breakthrough came when Watt designed the sun and planet motion in 1781. This enabled the engine to use a rotary motion. In 1782 the appearance of the double-acting rotary engine, to which was added a parallel motion in 1784 and a governor in 1788 to ensure smooth, regular operation, perfected the new driving power for the mills. The old, long, narrow mill buildings, constructed for hand machines, were no longer suitable for the larger steam driven ones and factories of a new design had to be constructed **(138)**.

The installation of a steam engine was a costly business as may be observed from a study of the specification of the engine to be installed in the mills of Richard Ingham at Todmorden, to carry a load of twenty-six horsepower. The erection of the engine on the site cost £16.10s board and lodging for three men from 8 January 1824 to 28

February when the engine commenced work. Ure **(139)** says the first cotton mill to be driven by steam was erected at Papplewick in 1785, followed by Peel's mill at Bury in 1787. Two years later Drinkwater's mill in Manchester and by 1790, Samuel Oldknow's mill had steam engines. The first Yorkshireman to use steam to drive his mills was Benjamin Gott, at Bean Ing mills, Leeds, where he installed a forty horsepower engine to drive his spinning frames. This was the largest engine in the county at that time **(88)**. Gott had capital available and built two mills at Holbeck, Leeds, where he was able to experiment **(89)**. He quickly found himself in competition with men like Fisher of Holbeck and Brook of Pudsey as well as Hirst of Leeds, the latter being the first man to use the mule for spinning woollen yarns **(52)**. Like his Lancashire neighbours, Gott found himself obliged to run night shifts to cope with the demand for spun yarn. The majority of these new manufacturers had started life as clothiers, whose industry made Leeds a manufacturing town.

Outside Leeds the introduction of the steam engine was slow, due to ancient tradition and opposition. When John Bradley wanted to install a steam engine in his Horton mill, Bradford in 1793, his workmen threatened to sue him for damages arising from the noise and smoke **(96)**. In 1800 there was only one steam engine in Huddersfield, according to the evidence given before the House of Lords by John Radcliffe, but W.B. Crump **(61)** states that there was an engine at Cocking Steps mill, Netherton in 1801 which cost £200. Morehouse **(109)** asserts that in 1798 steam engines were used to drive the scribbling mills at Holmfirth. By and large the first use of the steam engine was to supplement the water supply in time of drought.

Erik Svedenstjerna, touring England in 1802 **(107)**, was surprised to find steam engines more widely used than water or wind mills in Sweden. According to Lord **(102)** there were 321 engines at work which were built by Boulton and Watt between 1775 and 1800. English **(70)** believes that the reason for the slow change to steam was due to the shortage of engine tenters who were skilled boilermen as well. Carelessness often led to serious accidents, as happened at Ashton-under-Lyne when a mill boiler exploded in 1846, killing several people and demolishing part of the mill and several houses **(9)**.

The expansion of the steam-driven mill brought the era of the mill chimneys, standing like forests of tall trees. William Lever of Bolton, later Lord Leverhulme, said that mill chimeys had improved the northern landscape. Paul Mantoux **(107)** points out that the introduction of the steam engine made possible the development of large-scale industry. Factories were no longer confined to the valleys, in some isolated places close to a stream, for the canal system enabled coal to be brought at cheap rates to the mills. In due course the factories moved closer to the coalfields and the centres of population, so giving rise to the black industrial Victorian 'toadstools' **(58)**. It is important to emphasise, as Mantoux does, that coal was not suddenly discovered in the eighteenth century as a fuel for factories, but that it had played an important part in the economy before Watt's improvements. The clothiers had used coal to boil the water in their dyehouses, which they were now converting into scribbling mills, for sizing warps and steaming weft. The engine house was an extension to the mill and in the early days the method of driving the machines was by an upright vertical shaft, driving pairs of noisy bevel gears and broad leather belts. The engine house was the pride of the engine tenter who kept the entire room spotlessly clean, with the brass and steel work on the engine in a highly polished state **(82)**.

In the early days the machines were constructed from wood, with the essential brass and iron parts made by the local blacksmith. The steam engine created the need for machines constructed of iron and accurately fitted to make them capable of running at higher speeds than when driven by water power. A very clumsy comb, to be driven by steam, was designed by Thomas Cartwright of Doncaster who named it 'Big Ben', after a popular boxer. In 1794 James Garnet brought the mule to Bradford, and Ramsbotham the comb. The town of Bradford, at that time, was a small place where grass grew in the streets. By 1804 there were several large mills in the town and the demand for raw wool denuded the old textile areas of East Anglia of their supplies of raw wool **(96)**. The first two decades of the nineteenth century saw the appearance of the first of those specialist firms known as textile machine makers, and amongst them such names as Dobson and Barlow, Butterworth and Dickinson of Burnley, George Hattersley and Prince-Smith of Keighley.

The small man saw the new factories as a threat to his livelihood, and in 1780 a petition was presented to the House of Commons to check the expansion of machines, arguing that their product was inferior to that of hand-production, but the petition failed. Doring Ramsbotham wrote a pamphlet pointing out that the troubles caused by the introduction of machines were of a transitory nature **(119)**. In 1794 when a similar petition was again presented to Parliament a Bill was introduced to protect these men but it was thrown out in the same way as the Bill to enforce the old Elizabethan apprenticeship regulations of 1563. The government was no longer prepared to favour domestic industry at the expense of the new factories, for an enquiry made in 1803 revealed that only ten per cent of the cloth sold was woven on power looms, the rest being produced by the clothiers, who survived as hand loom weavers until the mid-century **(14)**.

In Lancashire objections to machines had been raised as early as 1769, arising from the fear that the new machines would destroy the livelihood of the domestic cotton workers. When the Blackburn spinners destroyed Hargreaves's spinning jennies, an Act was passed by Parliament that riots to destroy machines constituted an offence punishable by death. Despite the Act, riots spread and by 1779 were more serious. Josiah Wedgwood described in a letter to Thomas Bentley how he met an advance party of rioters at Chowbent, on their way from Bolton to destroy Birkacre mill at Chorley. Being repulsed at the first attempt on the Saturday, they returned on the following Monday, about 8,000 strong and marched on the mill. The premises were defended by Sir Richard Arkwright and fifty men, but they were soon outnumbered by the attackers who destroyed not only the mill, but the contents also **(6)**.

The details of the damage caused were reported to Quarter Sessions, where the leaders of the attack were tried and sentenced, but the punishments were not severe by the standards of the age **[doc. 26]**. The reason for this was the attitude of the middle class, which feared the new machines would reduce wages and so increase the poor rates, so that they were as hostile to machinery as were the operatives. Further attempts to destroy Robert Peel's mill at Altham ended with the death sentence being passed on many rioters. This was emphasised in a resolution passed by the Lancashire justices in Quarter Sessions, welcoming the new machines as a source of employment for the poor **[doc. 27]** and claiming that if the use of these should be prohibited then foreign countries would benefit. Arkwright made no attempt to rebuild his mill at Birkacre and surrendered the lease **(122)**.

As the cotton industry expanded and employment increased, the attitude to the new ideas changed. However, in the woollen industry with its older traditions, change was more difficult and there were riots in Leeds in 1780, although the jenny was welcomed by the small clothier as a new weapon to protect his independence **(89)**. The introduction of the gig mill into Wiltshire and Somerset in 1802 caused riots among the woollen weavers in these counties **(33)**. Evidence is available which reveals that by 1793 complete spinning mills were offered for sale as complete units **[doc. 28]**. In the same year the clothiers in the city were offering their congratulations to Thomas Lloyd for building a new fulling mill in Armley **[doc. 29]**.

Men hated not only the machine but also the factory. To those who were accustomed to working at home or in a small loom shop, the factory discipline seemed harsh. Though the hours worked in domestic industry were long, a man could select his working hours according to his preference. He would come and go as he pleased, or be idle for two or three days each week. The relationships between employer and employee were personal and not bound by rigid rules and regulations (23). The domestic worker saw little difference between the mill and going to prison or to an army barracks. Hence the early manufacturers found it difficult to obtain labour, as did David Dale at New Lanark mills.

What eased the situation was the existence of a floating population moving into the towns from the overlarge families in the countryside, but not, as is so often erroneously assumed, part of a mass exodus rising from enclosures. The new factories attracted workers from the poorest areas of the country, including Ireland and the Scottish highlands. The attraction of industry for these people was the fact that the cotton trade offered more opportunities and better earnings than the old system. The textile industry in all its branches, except dyeing and finishing, was suitable for women and children. Their nimble fingers and natural dexterity made them suitable as pieceners for joining broken threads on the mule or water frame. In addition child labour was cheap, being about one-third the cost of adult labour plus food and lodgings (132).

The easiest method was to obtain children from the town workhouses. The number of children on the hands of the London parish overseers increased rapidly in the second half of the eighteenth century as the result of an Act promoted by Jonas Hanway. This Act compelled the overseers of the poor to board out pauper children and pay the nurse a bonus for each one that survived (57). Before this Act few pauper children lived long enough to be a nuisance to society. The Hammonds point out (87) that the requirements of the large town workhouses and the needs of the factories created a situation comparable to that in the West Indian plantations. Just as the Spanish employers in America wanted imported labour because native labour was in short supply, so the new factories in the remote valleys were in the same situation. The workhouses were a source of child labour in some quantity and they served the Lancashire cotton mills as the Guinea coast served the West Indies. Samuel Romilly, writing his memoirs in 1811, described their destiny [doc. 30]. Contracts were therefore drawn up between the overseers and the manufacturers, and children were shipped to the factories in lots varying from fifty to one hundred. They were then bound as apprentices by the Justices of the Peace for seven years, according to the Statute of Artificers of 1563.

These parish apprentices were, at first, the only children employed in the factories, for the local residents refused to send their own, having discovered the conditions (85). Richard Arkwright entered into contracts with the overseers of Clerkenwell for children from the poorhouses in 1796 (73). The apprenticeship of pauper children was not a new thing in the late eighteenth century. Such children had been sent out as apprentices under the Tudors (13). But the conditions under which many of these apprentices worked were disgraceful: their working day was often from sixteen to eighteen hours and some worked twenty-four hours per day, and accidents were frequent when the exhausted children had to continue working. When the Lancashire magistrates discovered the real conditions of employment, they issued an order at their Quarter Sessions of 1784 that in future they would sign no apprenticeship papers for children who were employed in the night or worked more than ten hours per day [doc. 31]. A rider was added to this that the notice should be published in the press and notification made to the Justices of the neighbouring counties. The manufacturers evaded this, as they did the Act of 1802 which forbade night work, by employing free children or non-indentured labour. The source of this supply was the children of those families which were badly affected by the outbreak of war in 1793 and were compelled to send their children to work to maintain the family (54).

Despite considerable research it appears to be a common opinion that the evils of child labour came from the new factories. In fact the evils of forced child labour were common under the domestic system. Daniel Defoe (2) described how the weavers employed children of four or five years of age in Halifax, commenting on it as thoroughly worth while. On the other hand, under the earlier system of apprenticeship the apprentice was educated as well as made into a craftsman, not a cog in an industrial machine as he later became. Cook-Taylor (58) states that the most exacting and harshest employers of labour were the parents. In so far as domestic industry was on a small scale, these deficiencies were well hidden, but in the large factory where all could see, then the evils inherited from the domestic system were intensified. The case of Robert Blincoe at Lowdham, and later at Linto mill, Nottingham is well known, for both Cooke-Taylor and Mantoux have recorded his experiences in some detail (57, 107).

Not every factory treated its apprentices in the same manner as Blincoe. When Samuel Greg built Quarry Bank mill at Styal, Manchester, in 1784 at a cost of £14,000, the population was but scanty, so it was necessary to import labour of two types. The first was from the workhouse, the apprentices being fed and clothed but not paid any wages; the second was the true apprentice who received from ninepence to one shilling and sixpence weekly. To these two was added a third, namely the free labour from the Cheshire parishes. At Quarry Bank the apprentices were housed in special buildings and their indentures reveal that the main sources of supply were Newcastle, Ashton-under-Lyne, Liverpool, London and Cheshire. There were forty-two boys and a number of girls lodged under the care of a master and mistress. Collier **(56)** has described in detail the care given to these apprentices. No more than two to a bed, the sheets changed monthly and the rooms washed at regular intervals. There was a complete new set of Sunday clothes every two years and working clothes as required. The diet was sufficient, being composed of oatmeal, milk, bread, boiled pork, beef and mutton, with pot beans and other vegetables. On Sunday mornings all attended church, in the afternoon the Sunday school, and the evening was free. All were taught to read and write, and the rules of arithmetic, and one night each week there was compulsory education for the boys in groups of eight. Apprentice labour was, therefore, when properly supervised, not so cheap as free labour. Some apprentices absconded out of sheer monotony and the urge to see their relatives.

Factories of this nature were not, as a rule, in the majority. Parliament, by the Act of 1792, empowered the Justices of the Peace to cancel apprenticeship indentures where there was evidence of ill-treatment by an employer (52 Geo. IIIc.5). On conviction the employer must pay the parish £10 or the family an indemnity of the same amount. Another Act in the following year made it possible for Justices to levy a fine on employers at their discretion, but since many Justices were also employers these Acts were rarely enforced. Indeed the factory with its dreadful conditions of vice and barbarity appeared to many as a hell. The writer of an article in the *Gentleman's Magazine* for 1802 described a Lancashire spinning mill as 'Hell's Gate' **(77)**.

The conditions of the factory buildings were a hazard to health. Rooms were low, with narrow windows that were nearly always closed, to economise on space. The carding rooms had an atmosphere heavily laden with fluff, making it probable that eventually lung diseases would develop in the operative. Where flax was spun the wet conditions caused the clothing of the employees to become saturated. The atmosphere was made more foul by the heavy smoke from the tallow candles **(133)**. It is of no surprise to discover that a virulent fever, closely resembling gaol fever, broke out in Radcliffe, near Manchester, in 1784. The fever affected entire families and was often fatal to the males. Beilby Porteus, Bishop of Chester, one of the few bishops who recognised the harmful effects of the factory conditions, studied the report of the Manchester doctors on the fever and made some comments on the findings that long hours, confined space and limited leisure had been the cause. In his *Letter to the Clergy of the Diocese of Chester on Sunday Schools* written two years later, Porteus emphasised the essential need for leisure on Sundays (11). Unfortunately Porteus had too much faith in the manufacturers to reform their system on a voluntary basis and nothing was done.

Those who survived the stresses and strains of the factory system were stunted, deformed and mutilated as well as ignorant and corrupt. They had received little education and little technical training, only sufficient to enable them to perform a routine process, and therefore unable to take up any other employment, which made them virtually factory slaves. Adult workers were not treated so badly as the apprentices and free children but in their turn adults suffered from long hours, overcrowded mills, objectionable foremen and employers (12). The basic cause of the trouble was the uncontrolled power of the capitalist, whose responsibility was confined to the payment of wages for work done and nothing else. If such were the conditions of the spinning mills and their labour force what was the position of the hand loom weavers (149)?

According to Thompson (134) a certain amount of myth has surrounded the status of the hand loom weaver, but Daniels (62) points out that weavers were a prosperous community when abundant supplies of yarn became available. As more cotton yarn came on the market the weaving of wool and linen in Lancashire almost ceased. Since weaving was still a domestic craft, and the demand for cotton cloth seemed insatiable, barns, cart sheds, and outbuildings were altered to make loom shops. New weavers' cottages with loom shops attached were built and the price of labour rose five times to as much as £5 per week. The petitions to Parliament from the weavers, during the eighteenth century, do not reveal the existence of independent weavers, but rather of small farmers who were also weavers. The *Manchester Mercury* (10) advertised small farms with loom shops attached as being for sale. Aiken, describing the country around Manchester (22) in 1795, says that farms in the Middleton area were from twenty to thirty acres in size and occupied by weavers, but in Rochdale the farms were small and rarely brought in more than £70 per annum. The decline of the yeoman is, for Aiken, the time when he ceased to farm and became a full time weaver. He classifies the weavers into two groups, the first being those who work in houses or cellars in the large towns, and the second, as those who live in scattered hamlets carrying out two occupations.

Gaskell **(87)** in his description of the manufacturing population of England idealises the eighteenth century weaving communities, and Engels visualises an idealistic setting for the grandparents of the factory operatives of his day **(55)**. William Marcroft, writing of his family at Rochdale, described the prosperity of the silk weaver **(97)** where there were several members of the family engaged in weaving as a unit. To rectify this apparently ideal picture, Thompson **(134)** rightly points out that the weavers of Norwich and the south-west were not so fortunate as their northern contemporaries, and in any case weavers' prosperity depended to a great extent on the quality and type of fabric being woven. John Makin **(4)** giving evidence before the select committee on hand loom weavers in 1833, pointed out that the muslin weavers of Bolton dressed like gentlemen in top boots and ruffled shirts, carried a cane and were able to afford to hire a coach. French **(74)** in his *Life of Crompton*, states that the muslin weavers walked about with a five pound note in their hatbands and smoked long churchwarden pipes. This is probably correct, for the weaving of fine fabrics like muslin demanded a high degree of skill. Over in Oldham, where coarser fabrics were woven, weavers expressed concern at the numbers flocking to enter the craft without having served an apprenticeship, and resolved to limit entry to the trade to prevent a reduction in their standard of living [**doc. 32**]. Similar meetings were held in other cotton towns so that the magistrates became afraid that riots would occur, and on 11 September 1781 they forbade gatherings of weavers to protest at the dilution of the trade [**doc. 33**] **(42)**.

The attraction for immigrant labour was weaving and not spinning, so Bolton, Rochdale, Mottram, Middleton and Oldham became the meccas of those who believed they could earn high wages as weavers, but many were disillusioned. According to Collier **(56)** weavers were always in a weak position because of the small amount of fixed capital required to operate in their home while their employer's capital was invested in materials. Since weavers had no capital reserves for hard times they reduced their prices for weaving, when trade was bad. In times of prosperity a man could buy a loom for £2 and become a weaver, for at such times it was easy to earn a living weaving plain cloth, hence the ranks of the weavers tended to become diluted. Collier states that the majority of the weavers, such as those weaving fustians and smallware, earned modest wages, while those weaving checks, muslins and cambrics received high wages. Those who confined themselves to weaving calico and coarse cloth were very poorly paid. The real peak of prosperity for the hand loom weaver in Lancashire was from 1770 to 1800 when many abandoned farming for full-time weaving. The decline in hand loom weaving began about 1797 and those who remained in the trade ended their lives in dire poverty. The impact of the Napoleonic wars and the subsequent depression caused a reduction in prices. Further, the power loom had been improved for weaving plain cloth, so by 1813 the weavers of Bolton and Preston had to petition the magistrates for assistance, but all was in vain. The day of the independent weaver was finished [doc. 34].

In the West Riding, matters were somewhat different. The sub-division of the wool trade and the slow adoption of the power loom enabled some clothiers to continue for fifty years, and in the districts manufacturing pile fabric the hand loom weaver survived until the Second World War. Although the clothiers and croppers of the West Riding had petitioned Parliament to enforce a seven years apprentice-ship, which the factory owners had abandoned, there appears to have been no opposition to the factory as such in Huddersfield, although there was opposition to the introduction of the mechanical shearing frames.

A resolution of the master clothiers of Saddleworth, Honley and Kirkburton maintained that the domestic system was the one most suited to the area, but proposed that the number of looms should be limited to five per clothier, with 160 spindles the maximum for spinning and a full seven years apprenticeship made compulsory. Crump (61) believes that the absence of opposition in the Huddersfield area was due to the fact that Huddersfield was concentrating on fancy goods and very fine cloth, so it was left to the croppers to protest about machines. Joseph Lawson writing about Pudsey and weaving in 1826, pointed out the hardships faced by the hand loom weaver [doc. 35], and contrasted these with the advantages of power looms (101) which enabled the weaver to concentrate on his job and not have to undertake a multitude of odd tasks in addition.

By the turn of the century the northern industrial towns were pointed out as examples to the rest of the country. John Jones, a Manchester spinner, eulogised the status of cotton and Manchester [doc. 36]. There were also those who portrayed in folk song the poverty of the weaver and the slavery of the spinning mill [docs. 37, 49]. The point is that the weaving trade attracted large numbers at a time when hand loom weaving was beginning to decline. The select committee of 1806 recommended that the old legislation which restricted trade, in fact all those things which the weavers petitioned to retain, should be swept away in the interests of progress. The last obstacles being removed, the way was open in the textile industry for exploitation by uncontrolled capitalism, with some very ugly faces

Analysis

indeed in its ranks. Marx **(108)** believed that exploitation was shameless
for those made redundant by the changes and driven to cut-throat
competition to survive. Thompson **(134)** feels that future generations
gained by the sufferings of those subject to the changes, but for the
sufferers this comfort was very cold.

PART THREE

Assessment

5 Population and Towns

It is not the inventions themselves that are the sole important point for consideration: their effects on people, their earnings, the cost of living and the communities in which they dwelt, must also be given attention. It was the combination of all these factors, together with the effect of technical improvements, that led in the long term to the factory reform movements of the 1830s.

According to Arthur Young (18) industry and population go together. Hence industrial areas are populous in proportion to their degrees of industry and Mantoux (107) produces evidence to support this view. By the last decade of the eighteenth century the factory system was in being, the factory operatives were emerging as a class, and the industrial centres were expanding rapidly. The reasons for this sudden expansion are not altogether clear. George (78) has made an attempt to analyse the factors but it must be remembered that the growth of population is a modern development which may change again in the foreseeable future. The increase in population led to a migration to new areas. In 1700 the area of high density was south of a line drawn from Bristol to East Anglia, an area which contained about three-fifths of the population. The northern regions were thinly populated, having a range of 80 to 110 persons to the square mile.

By 1760 the pattern was changing and the population was expanding rapidly, especially in the Midlands, Lancashire, the West Riding, Durham and Northumberland. Beilby Porteus, Bishop of Chester from 1776 to 1787, speaking in the House of Lords during a debate on the numbers of Roman Catholics in England in 1781, stated that the population of his diocese of Chester had increased by 250,000 during the previous fifty years (21). There seems to be no doubt that the factory system saw the creations of those conurbations which have not even now ceased to grow, but which continue to spread over the countryside. Before the era of the steam engine, the early mills had to be close to a town for market purposes, and for communications. A supply of labour was essential, not only for the mill, but also for those ancillary processes that were carried out in the home and without which the spinning mill could not operate.

Assessment

The earliest textile towns to develop were the cotton towns, of which Manchester became the most important. Aiken (22) points out that Manchester was already ancient in 1700, situated on the Irwell, close to its confluence with the Mersey. A coarse type of woollen cloth called 'cotton' was woven there and fancy goods were also produced for export to Africa by the Liverpool merchants. According to a town census of 1757, the population of Manchester was 20,000, but the figure returned to Bishop Porteus at his primary visitation was 30,000 (21). Salford, which was then counted as part of Manchester, covered an area somewhat less than the present Victoria railway station, without the old Exchange station. The area round Cannon Street and Deansgate was one of narrow lanes and shops in 1730, but all this was changed following the opening of the Bridgewater canal, from Worsley to Manchester, followed by the Mersey canal. The canals meant that supplies of cheap coal could be brought to the town and better communication was provided to Liverpool, leading to commercial expansion. In 1786 Sir Richard Arkwright built the first cotton spinning mill in the town and from that date onwards the population increased rapidly from 30,000 in 1778 to 95,000 in 1801 (137). In that year there were fifty spinning mills driven by steam engines which Axon describes so effectively (30).

No town planning of any kind existed, so houses were built in long rows close to the mills and crowded together with as many houses per acre as could be crammed in. The insanitary crowded conditions created epidemics which J. Ferriar described in his report to the Board of Health in Manchester in 1805 (72). According to J.P. Kay, who wrote of the moral and physical conditions in Manchester in 1832 (99), the operatives lived in the centre of the town in a maze of streets round Canal Street with alleys stretching all the way from Piccadilly to Ardwick Green. The houses he saw, Kay condemned as unfit for human habitation even in his day.

Ashton, in his guide to Manchester (26), stated that wells were the only source of drinking water and these were badly contaminated. In the Ancoats area the inhabitants had to find water wherever they could. The houses had neither gardens nor yards, so this created a problem for the drying of clothes since a by-law of 1792 forbade the stretching of clothes lines across the streets. The better-class folk had rainwater tubs to augment their supplies. The manufacturers moved to the outskirts and built themselves villas and houses suitable for their position. William Ogden, the perpetual curate of Ardwick, writing to the Bishop of Chester in 1831, in response to an enquiry about poor persons, stated that there were no poor in his parish since it was a residential area for respectable city business men. The problems of housing and sanitation were intensified, not only by the influx of labour from neighbouring areas but also by the Irish immigrants who came over seeking good regular wages.

Manchester was not the only town to expand. Edwin Butterworth (42) described how Oldham grew following the opening of the first cotton mill in 1776 and how, twelve years later, there were twenty-five spinning mills and a population of 20,000. When French (74) wrote about Bolton in 1753 he described it as a one street village. The vicar, in his report to Bishop Porteus in 1778 [doc. 23] described the problems he saw resulting from the industrial expansion, and by 1890 it is possible to see the town fully developed with a rigid social structure and many social problems [doc. 38].

The building of a six-storey mill at Tydesley in 1780 changed it from a hamlet of two farms and eight cottages into a village of 162 houses and 976 souls (22). In the woollen districts growth was slower. Leeds did not expand substantially until after 1793 when the first mills appeared. By 1801 there were 53,000 inhabitants, but nearly one-half lived outside the town itself and by 1820 a housing problem had already appeared in the Kirkgate side of the town (60). Halifax changed but little, it remained for a long time a town of small manufacturers and domestic industry. James Smith, in his report to a parliamentary commission (1), pointed out that in 1760 Halifax contained about 50,000 persons. The population reached 63,000 forty years later and it remained an area where poverty, immorality and promiscuity were widespread. The old clothing areas of Norwich, Tiverton and Exeter could not compete with the northern mills and fell into decline and decay to become attractive tourist centres by the twentieth century.

6　Wages and Prices

F.M. Eden, writing on the state of the poor in 1797 **(68)**, described the situation of the factory worker as a person with only his labour to offer in exchange for wages and whose daily needs meant daily labour to satisfy them, so he was always at the mercy of the employer. This situation was by no means a new one in 1797, for it had appertained before amongst the weavers of the south-west and the stocking knitters of Nottingham, both of whom were at the mercy of the clothiers who gave out the work. The new factory owner was more powerful than the old clothier in his ability to force terms on his employees. Although Thorold Rogers **(120)** in his history of prices based his conclusions on agriculture rather than industry, something in the industrial field has been undertaken by G. Unwin **(138)**, T.S. Ashton **(28)**, and the Hammonds **(86)**. Nevertheless, a comprehensive survey of wages in industry, based on business records, needs to be undertaken before any accurate judgment can be made, for wages varied so widely from area to area that any comments can only be an approximate assessment at this stage.

On the subject of wages, one important point is clear and is emphasised by W. Bowden **(36)**, who asserts that the earnings of the industrial worker were higher than those of his counterpart in agriculture. According to Arthur Young **(18)** a cotton weaver of 1770 could earn from 7 to 10 shillings each week in Manchester, while a Leeds woollen weaver earned 8s and a Witney blanket weaver 11s. Wool combers, with their small numbers and high skills, could easily earn a wage of 13s; the worst paid were the stocking knitters of Nottingham, whose net earnings were about 4s, weekly.

Wages rose between 1770 and 1795 when the cotton spinners in the mills could earn about 16s weekly and the muslin printers as much as 25s. These wages were attractive to the rural resident and exerted strong pressure to move to the towns **(104)**. A study of the reports in the Commons Journals show that following the invention of the spinning jenny and the water frame, there was a shortage of both looms and weavers. By 1792 the calico weavers could earn from 15 to 20s a week while the velvet and muslin weavers earned about 80s **(1)**. In the following year the Bolton manufacturers, in order to reduce unemployment, limited the supply of work to 10s a week per weaver. Hence from a wage of £4 per piece of velvet in 1792, the same weaver received 55s in 1792 and 36s in 1800. As their earnings fell, so the length of the woven piece was increased from forty to fifty yards.

S. Chapman (53) believes the reason for this fall in earnings was not the introduction of the power loom, which was never mentioned in the petitions to Parliament, but the overcrowding of the weaving market by country labourers accustomed to low wages and willing to accept the conditions laid down by the manufacturers. F.M. Eden (68) points out that in 1796 a Leeds woollen weaver could earn 18s a week, while the best weavers were able to earn a reasonable wage and maintain a good standard of living because they wove on piece rates, yet it was at the expense of the less able who joined the ranks of the unemployed. Those who were hardest hit were the wool combers whose earnings had always been 60 per cent above those of the weavers but now fell to the level of the latter due to Cartwright's combing machines. The croppers, according to the Webbs (148), were also affected and vented their wrath in the Luddite riots of 1811 and 1812 (133).

The lowest wage earners were the women and children, the latter as 'free children' receiving about 4s weekly. Arthur Young (18) estimated that the women who spun yarn on the jenny could earn about 5s a week in 1778, which was no less than the earnings of 1770. The real threat to adult male labour came from the employment of children and women as a source of cheap labour, but as machines became more complicated and needed greater skill to tend them, the parish apprenticeship system had to terminate. Mantoux (107) says that the period of transition caused the greatest difficulties and suffering to individuals for years and has rightly deserved the curse of the ordinary man.

A great deal of the change occurred during a period of war and therefore under exceptional circumstances. From 1720 to 1765 was a period of prosperity when the working man became accustomed to wearing leather shoes and eating white bread. From 1765 to 1775 was a stable period but after the latter date the price of wheat rose suddenly to 66s per quarter. Bread riots took place in many areas and though prices fell slightly, the situation of the artisan was precarious when war broke out in 1793. The bad harvests of 1795 and 1796 caused wheat prices to rise to 108s per quarter, but the good harvests which followed led to wheat prices falling to 54s per quarter. Between 1799 and 1801 the succession of bad harvests led to the rise in the price of wheat to famine level at 128s.6d per quarter (19). An exhortation by the Privy Council in 1801 to ration the consumption of grain and bread was proclaimed in all areas. However the Peace of Amiens in 1802 was accompanied by improved harvests led to a fall in the price of wheat to 66s per quarter, but this was to last only a short time, for prices again increased when war was resumed. T. Carter **(45)** pointed out that, since beer was one shilling per gallon, meat at eight pence per pound and cheese at the same price, potatoes at 3s the bushel and the four-pound loaf of bread at 1s.2d it was difficult for the poor to live. Indeed the budget of a cotton spinner earning 25s a week in 1833 shows how little remained over for clothing and other items after food had been purchased [doc. 39]. In many instances families had to rely on the parish poor relief to help them out.

Alongside and closely connected with earnings and prices was what may be termed the state of trade. G.W. Daniels **(62)** gives the imports of raw cotton in 1783 as 9,735,633 lb, rising in the following ten years to 34,907,497 lb, showing how rapidly the industry had expanded as the result of the introduction of machinery. Unfortunately the aftermath of war of 1793 saw a number of bankruptcies with a great deal of unemployment arising from the depressed nature of the industry [doc. 40]. Not until the Peace of Amiens was there a revival in trade, and then only for a brief period, which encouraged the building of some new mills. The reopening of hostilities in May 1803 followed by the Continental System and the Berlin Decrees, depressed trade to such an extent that unemployment was rife. F. Collier **(56)** points out that there were numerous petitions to Parliament about the distress, but nothing was done.

The winter of 1808-09 was very severe and the poor were in such dire straits that the *Manchester Mercury* for 3 January 1809 devoted an entire article to the conditions of the poor in Ardwick and the efforts undertaken for their relief. The summer saw a slight improvement with exports to South America again possible but the following year was equally depressing. The blockade resulting from the Continental System impeded imports of food, and the outbreak of war with America in 1812 cut both supplies of raw cotton and trade with New England **(75)**. The price of food soared and in Heckmondwike the price of wheat reached 155s per quarter and at the same time unemployment increased and wages fell. Peel **(112)** believes that the Luddite riots were the result of low wages, high prices and unemployment. By November 1811 letters from Bolton implied that any increase in the price of food without a corresponding increase in wages would be disastrous and lead to trouble, yet within six months the prices of oatmeal, vital to the northern diet, and potatoes had doubled. Woollen cloth workers, like the cotton workers, were caught in the same unfortunate circumstances and struck blindly at what many believed were the causes of misery, namely the new machines **(63)**.

7 Luddite Riots

Sundry ideas were put forward as to the cause of the Luddite riots. The Duke of Newcastle believed the Luddites were financed by France to cause economic disaster. J. Lloyd of Stockport saw the Irish malcontents as fomenting disorder, while Gravener Henson of Nottingham considered the riots to be a government-inspired movement to give an excuse to impose military rule (133). In South Yorkshire the riots were regarded as the work of the Roman Catholics to aid the French [doc. 41]. It was, as M. Thomis points out (123), in Nottingham, where the hosiery and lace industries were oversubscribed and dependent on overseas markets which had virtually disappeared by 1811, that trouble occurred. The *Nottingham Review* for 6 December 1811 pointed out that it was not the machines in themselves that the rioters opposed; the use to which these machines were put was the real target.

In the West Riding it was the croppers who led the attack on machines, and also protested about increasing the number of apprentices admitted to the trade, who would augment the labour market and reduce wages. As early as 1803 the croppers at Benjamin Gott's mill in Leeds had struck on the apprentice question [doc. 42]. The new shearing frame was opposed on the grounds that it would reduce the demand for labour. In reality the frame was a pair of cropper's shears mounted on a travelling carriage, which is described and illustrated by W.B. Crump (61). Open hostility emerged on 19 January 1812 when Oatlands mill, Huddersfield, which contained the new cropping machines, was set on fire on the Sunday. Towards the end of February the finishing shops of Joseph Hirst and William Hinchliffe of Huddersfield were destroyed. In mid-March, the houses of John Garner at Honley and of Clement Dyson at Dungeon were attacked, and Francis Vickerman, who had thirty pairs of shears in his mills at Taylor Hill, Huddersfield, had them broken and his property destroyed (121). It took the rioters no more than twenty minutes to break forty pairs of shears at Rawdon mills, Leeds. The attack on the cropping shops of J. Smith at Snowgatehead and James Brook of Honley, both near Huddersfield on 5 April 1812, roused real alarm, as John Howson reported in his letter to his employer at Cannon Hall, Barnsley [doc. 43].

Up to this point it was the small men who had received attention. On 9 April a crowd of 600 men attacked Joseph Foster's mill at Horbury, Wakefield, and after some slight resistance managed to break in. The rioters did not break or damage any of the scribbling machines, only the cropping frames and apart from this only windows were broken. The plans made in John Wood's cropping shop at Longroyd Bridge, Huddersfield, culminated in the attack on Rawfolds mill of William Cartwright, which was near Liversedge, an attack so graphically described by Charlotte Brontë **(40)**. This was followed by another attack on the Ottiwell mill of William Horsfall at Marsden in the Colne Valley, on 27 April. Horsfall had developed the cropping frame to a high degree of efficiency, and, suspecting an attack, had his mill defended by the military armed with cannon. The soldiers repulsed the attack and in revenge the rioters laid an ambush for Horsfall and shot him on his way home. The tragedy caused the Horsfall family to abandon machine cropping and return to hand methods, but the family were so demoralised that they disposed of the mill shortly afterward. The incident is described by Dr Phyllis Bentley **(34)**. In Lancashire it was the steam loom that came under attack. On 20 March 1812 the mill of William Ratcliffe of Stockport was the first weaving mill to be attacked. This was followed by a series of riots on a large scale in Manchester, Oldham, Ashton-under-Lyne, Rochdale and Macclesfield. An attempt was made to destroy the mill of Daniel Burton at Middleton, resulting in seven deaths. The defence proved to be too strong for the attackers who contented themselves by burning Burton's house. The final episode was the destruction of Westhoughton mill, near Bolton, after a number of futile attempts **(133)**.

Evidence later given at the trials of the Luddites by persons who had been attacked show how widespread these riots were. Joseph Woodhead of Elland, near Halifax, was stopped by rioters who threatened to kill him but in the end contented themselves by firing shots over his head. Another witness, Thomas Broughton, a Barnsley weaver, described how he was admitted or, 'twisted in', as a Luddite and the plans that were made to achieve their ends [**doc. 44**]. According to Thompson there were not only weavers engaged in the riots but men of other occupations, and he quotes evidence of a joiner, a glazier and colliers in the mobs, so making these more than a mere weavers' or croppers' riot **(134)**. John Howson, writing to John Stanhope about the defence of Cannon Hall, pointed out that flour mills and threshing machines were also destroyed, thus indicating that food shortages were a further source of trouble [**doc. 45**]. In September 1812 Earl Fitzwilliam, the deputy lieutenant of the county of York, called for reports from the constables to establish the extent to which they patrolled and watched in their constabularies and investigated any associations or combinations which were illegal under the Anti-Combination Laws of 1800 [doc. 46].

There are problems attached to this episode of the Luddites. The Hammonds make their study of the *Skilled Labourer* read like a brief prepared for an attack by the Whigs in Parliament, with the intention to discredit the claim of authority that the movement was revolutionary, a view also expressed by Thompson (134). F.O. Darvill (63) points out that it was a dispute between men and their employers, but Thompson (134) considers that any evidence concerning the organisation of Luddism is tainted, since we only know of the existence of oath taking from rumour and the confession of prisoners. He sees Luddism as a form of working-class culture destined to lead to greater political awareness. Thomis (133) doubts the value to the historian of the concept of working-class culture and finds no other evidence beyond some working-class people acting illegally and presenting a challenge to society. It is difficult to agree that Luddism was a new pattern of working-class behaviour which influenced its participation in industry and politics. Asa Briggs (37) suggests that Luddism was one of the events that marked changes in the industrial structure of the country and that fluctuation in trade meant fluctuation in earnings, a matter which seemed of more importance than the Napoleonic Wars. Thompson (134) sees that where Luddism was defeated it changed to a move for parliamentary reform, but even that demand fluctuated with prosperity or poverty.

The revival in trade after 1813 lasted only for two years and 1816 was another disastrous year. Food was at famine prices and there was unrest in the north, coupled with a demand for reform. The distress culminated in the tragedy of Peterloo in 1819 (38) and Axon (30) describes the situation in Manchester at this time. Nevertheless, in the West Riding the manufacture of superfine cloth for the export market was being developed with great success by 1818 (144). There was a revival in trade in 1820 and the *Manchester Guardian* for 16 June 1821 described the well-dressed working class who attended the Whitsuntide races; but in the same edition there was a report of the uncertain trading conditions.

Financial problems on a large scale came in 1824. More than seventy banks failed, bringing bankruptcy to many manufacturers. Riots and machine breaking broke out again and from 1825 and 1833 no mills were built in Manchester and very few outside (56). The working man came off badly since he depended upon the ability or inability of the employer to cope with the situation. Indeed the weavers' riots in Barnsley in 1829 show how desperate were conditions for the textile operatives [doc. 47]. It is against this background and the problems raised by the growth of towns, the increasing mechanisation of industry, the incidence of war with its aftermath of unrest, that the next episode is set, that of factory reform with its violent protagonists fighting for or against change.

8 Factory Reform

The French Revolution and its excesses caused great concern to the British government in case it spread to this country. Fear of violent revolution became more important than the conditions in factories. The evils of child labour increased and many appeals were made to humanity on their behalf, but nothing was done until Sir Robert Peel, himself a manufacturer, unexpectedly took up the matter of factory conditions. Peel introduced a Bill into the Commons, which in 1802 became an Act for the Preservation of the Health and Morals of Apprentices and others employed in cotton mills. The provisions of the Act were limited and in the main were designed merely to reduce the hours of labour to twelve per day, exclusive of meals, and to abolish night labour for children. Further, every apprentice must receive some education during part of the day, attend church and receive religious instruction. The Justices of Peace were empowered to appoint visitors to factories to see the terms of the Act were carried out, but many of the magistrates were factory owners so nothing was done. The effect of the Act was to abolish the system of parish apprentices. The rotary steam engine had enabled factories to be built in the towns and to be staffed by free 'children', not parish apprentices. As the former were not bound by the terms of the Act, so the barbarous system of child labour continued. The system of factory apprentices was continued at the Styal mill of Robert Gregg until 1834 (56).

The evils continued, and by 1815 Peel managed to get a Royal Commission appointed to see if the provisions of the Act of 1802 could not be extended to every class of factory child. A mass of evidence was produced over the next two years. Nathaniel Gould, a Manchester merchant, and John Moss, a mill manager from Backbarrow, produced some vital evidence on child labour (80). In February 1818 a disastrous fire destroyed a cotton mill at Colnebridge, Huddersfield, in which seventeen children lost their lives, and the news of this disaster aroused much criticism. At this time the debate on a new factory Act was taking place and the Colnebridge incident was mentioned in the debate [doc. 48].

The result was the Factory Act of 1819 which forbade the

employment of children under nine years of age in a cotton mill and laid down that none between the age of nine and sixteen were to work more than twelve hours a day. Once again the terms of the Act concerned working hours in cotton mills only although the conditions in many woollen and linen mills were just as bad. In any case there were no provisions in the Act for compulsory enforcement of its conditions. The Act was amended in 1825 under Sir John Hobhouse, when the working hours on Saturdays were reduced from twelve to nine, and penalties were imposed for overworking. Again the weakness of the Act was the lack of provision for enforcement: there was no evidence of the real age of the children, as compulsory registration of births was not in force, and lastly there was no proper system of inspection of factories (113). The effect of Hobhouse's Act encouraged James Doherty, Thomas Daniel and Philip Grant of Manchester to work for further reform, but they received many setbacks until two West Riding men, one a manufacturer and the other an estate agent, give them fresh hope. It was the action of John Wood and Richard Oastler that gave a new impetus to factory reform (66).

In the 1820s the ideas of Robert Owen were considered to be a solution to the industrial problems. His successful experiments at New Lanark mills were much to the fore (111) and his idea of 'villages of cooperation' was adopted by later industrialists. One of these was Sir Titus Salt, who created the model industrial community at Saltaire. Owen did realise that the workers needed education before they could conduct village affairs, but this was a long-term project. For a time those with money and power gave him support, but his attacks on the monetary system, the profit motive, competitive industry and religion alienated many of his supporters, including those churchmen who had shown interest. The radicals showed little concern for Owen's proposals or for the campaigns by the revived trade unions for industrial action; political reform dominated their interests. Politicians, as usual, saw their interests best served by organising those who wanted to change one set of oppressive conditions for another, but to give them no choice in the selection. Those who sacrificed politics to industry and commerce were not those best fitted to decide the issues that confronted the country (79).

The campaign for further reform was conducted against a campaign for the reform of Parliament. It was a worsted manufacturer, John Wood of Horton Hall, Bradford, who originated the movement for a ten-hour day. Supported by two other manufacturers, John Rand and Matthew Thompson, he had attempted without success to get the rest of the Bradford manufacturers to accept his proposals. A chance visit to

Horton Hall by Richard Oastler, the agent to the Thornhills of Fixby Hall, gave Wood his opportunity. When Oastler left the house it was his firm intention to campaign against the factory system and reduce working hours (59). The condition of the children employed in the flax mills of John Marshall of Leeds had already been the subject of an attack in the election of 1826 [doc. 49] but the real explosion came on 16 October 1830. On that day Oastler's famous letter on Yorkshire slavery was published in the *Leeds Mercury*, a letter in which Oastler compared the system in the West Riding mills to Negro slavery in the plantations [doc. 50]. This was supported by a letter from John Wood on 27 October 1830.

The issue of the *Leeds Mercury* for 8 November 1830 contained a report from Richard Webster of Halifax describing conditions in the mills of that town [doc. 51] stressing the lack of time for food. The great body of mill owners in the West Riding and the linen weaving areas of Scotland were determined to block any legislation if they could do so. On 5 March 1831 a meeting of Halifax manufacturers, under the chairmanship of James Ackroyd, was held at the Old Cock Inn. They passed a resolution against any reduction in hours of work on the grounds that it would reduce wages, affect the export trade adversely, and create unemployment [doc. 52]. In the autumn of 1831 Sir John Hobhouse and Lord Morpeth introduced a Bill to limit the hours of work for children to 11½ in the day and 8½ on Saturdays, with proper breaks for meals and to cover all types of textile factories. To give encouragement to this Bill, 'short-time committees' were formed in Leeds, Huddersfield, Bradford and Manchester, as well as in other centres (95). Membership cut across party politics and these Committees used a variety of methods to put their case across to the public.

The opposition proved to be too powerful, so that Hobhouse's Bill was modified in committee, restricting its application to cotton mills only. It had the effect of abolishing night work and preventing the custom of having two sets of workers employed on alternate shifts in appalling conditions, but the provisions of the Act were often evaded. The issue of factory reform was bedevilled by the situation surrounding the issues of parliamentary reform and since a furious campaign was raging over the Reform Bill, the matter of factory reform receded into the background (38). Professor Trevelyan (136) saw two forces at work, the landlord and the millowner, engaged in a bitter struggle. McCord (105) stated that the real opponents of factory reform were the members of the Anti-Corn Law League, which said the Corn Laws made the reduction of working hours impossible.

Stirring meetings were held in factory towns where crowds varying from 12,000 to 18,000 were often present. In Bradford, Huddersfield and Leeds some of the manufacturers gave assistance, but at Halifax the opposition was tough. In Halifax the opposition received strong support from Edward Baines, the editor of the *Leeds Mercury*, who hated Oastler and his campaign and attacked him bitterly **(8)**. The *Leeds Intelligencer*, a radical paper, gave full support to the reform movement **(7)**. It pointed out the glaring contrasts between the mansions of the wealthy manufacturers and the poor hovels of the factory hands, forecasting some national disaster if the factory system continued unreformed. The opposition, as expected, came from vested interests which could always adapt a suitable current philosophy to suit and form a justification for their action.

Two clear attitudes have now emerged. The millowners presented the case that factory reform would reduce incomes, since to reduce the hours of labour for children and therefore of adults would reduce their earnings. Since many parents relied on the earnings of their children to support the family, this would be disastrously hard. Furthermore the millowners had good propaganda agencies which used the fact that Parson Bull and Oastler were Tories to arouse suspicion as to their true motives. The reformers for their part argued that work would be shared among more people, and since trade was increasing so should incomes. The working class had many critics who lumped them together indiscriminately, just as in our own day people from slum clearance areas have been stated, without exception, to have stored coals in the bathroom **(113)**.

Michael Sadler, the member for Newark, came forward in support of the Ten Hours movement and he was selected as spokesman in the House of Commons for the reformers. Unfortunately neither Sadler nor his supporter, Lord Morpeth, had any knowledge of the manufacture of cloth, so the opposition could attack them with ease. Although organisations for reform were strong in Yorkshire and Lancashire, yet the manufacturers in these areas obtained support from those in the less well organised districts of the west of England and Scotland. The Liberal press, especially the *Leeds Mercury*, the *Manchester Guardian* and the *Morning Chronicle*, came out on the side of the manufacturers. The reformers had the support of the *Edinburgh Review. Leeds Intelligencer* and the *Manchester Mercury* [doc. 53].

The propaganda of the reformers had some effect in that it was able to harness the support of 'respectable' people. The Society for the Improvement of the conditions of the Factory Children, gained the full support of the Duke of Sussex, the Earl of Feversham, the Lord Mayor of London and many others. Further support for Sadler was organised in the spring of 1832, which culminated in a mass meeting of textile workers in York on Easter Monday, addressed by Bull, Oastler, Wood and Sadler (119). In Lancashire, Dr J. Kay, who had given a grim description in his report, concerning life and death in Manchester, was one of the few doctors who supported the factory system; the majority were on the side of the reformers (99). At the same time Archbishop Howley presented a petition in the House of Lords which he had received from his parish of Rochdale concerning reform (73). The opposition claimed that Sadler's remarks were exaggerated and that the manufacturers could easily counter the allegations before a committee, so the Bill was referred to such a body. The proceedings of the commissioners fill a whole volume and the evidence took the greater part of a year to amass (4).

Unfortunately for Sadler the Reform Bill received the royal assent in 1832 and Parliament was dissolved. Sadler had been member for Newark, a borough which was disfranchised by the Act. In the general election that followed Sadler offered to stand for Leeds or Huddersfield but was rejected, although Manchester reformers sent a petition to Leeds asking that Sadler be adopted as their candidate, but all in vain. A successor was found in Lord Ashley, later seventh Earl of Shaftesbury, who agreed to reintroduce Sadler's Bill in 1833. Robert Southey had reported on the conditions of employment he had found in Marshall's flax mills in Leeds (118) so the opposition was expected to be strong. Marshall and Macaulay, the members for Leeds, Fenton of Huddersfield and Wood of Halifax were violently opposed to any change, and there were many in the new government who disliked interference in industry and would willingly listen to the opposition. Hence the, 'Association of Master Manufacturers' applied itself most energetically to the task of opposing factory reform. The chief spokesman for the manufacturers was Wilson Patten, who proposed a Royal Commission be appointed to enquire into the employment of children in factories. The reformers regarded that as another method to defeat intervention by the government. A commission to investigate and report upon factory conditions and employment was set up in London. It was to be fed with information collected by groups of assistant commissioners working locally who were to question people on factory conditions (80). The Short Time Committees organised demonstrations for the Ten Hours Bill wherever and whenever the commissioners appeared.

The arrival of the commissioners in Manchester was heralded by a demonstration of factory children in St Peter's Fields. They marched through the town carrying banners with inscriptions, 'A Muzzle for the

Steam Giant', and 'Ten Hours Bill and no Surrender' and following the meeting a petition was handed in at the York Hotel, King Street, for the commissioners [doc. 54]. Evidence was taken from Ralph Stanley the master of Gorton workhouse, who was convinced that the factory system was not harmful when compared with other trades such as calico printing, and another witness Joseph Hunt referred to the many deformed children in Manchester. For the employers, Henry Ashworth of Macclesfield stated he would not extend nor invest any further capital in his mills if hours were reduced, since profits would disappear (80).

The commissioners were greeted in Leeds by posters placed in prominent positions headed, APPROACH OF THE ENEMY [doc. 55] (144). On 6 June the commissioners received a vigorous protest in Bradford, while Dr Robert Chalmers was disturbed by the demonstration in Huddersfield which burned the commissioners in effigy on 22 June 1833 [doc. 56]. Another meeting on 1 July at Wibsey, Bradford, expressed disgust at the report (8). Manufacturers had to report on conditions in their mills, and to this end members of short-time committees observed the mills to be inspected to see if any 'window dressing' took place. E. Royston Pike (123) has supplied abundant evidence from the report on the evils of child labour, but not all factories were so bad as is commonly depicted. The evidence of John Sutcliffe of Skircoat, Halifax and Joshua Robinson of Smithy Place, Brockholes gives a very different impression (4).

On 17 June 1833 the Bill received a second reading, to limit the working hours to ten per day. It was reinforced by a petition organised by John Doherty, Oastler and Wood that the ten hour limit should apply to all below the age of eighteen. Lord Althorp, under pressure from the Whigs and millowners despite Ashley's opposition, received a majority to send the Bill to a select committee. Ashley thereupon handed the Bill over to Althorp and the result was the Factory Act of 1833.

J.C. Gill (73) states that the Act of 1833 in its original form was unacceptable to the vested interests of the manufacturers and others. He admits that the Whigs wanted, and got, Ashley's Bill improved. Professor Trevelyan (125) seems certain that the government wanted legislation in this field, but was unwilling to sacrifice the support of the manufacturer. Both do stress that the appointment of factory inspectors was an important step, but this would only be effective if the magistrates were prepared to convict. The problems arising from the defiance of the employers and the willingness of magistrates to impose minimum fines for breaches of the Act occurred in Blackburn,

Manchester and Leeds, as the report of the inspector on the mills of Taylor, Ibbotson & Co of Dewsbury clearly reveals [doc. 57]. Oastler, in a blistering letter to Edward Baines, attacked the miserable petty fine imposed on Joseph Schofield of Huddersfield, 'a deacon of Ramsden Street Chapel', for his wilful breaches of the Act.

The campaigners for the Ten Hours Bill continued their efforts, and on 23 June 1836 the member for Ashton-under-Lyne, C. Hindley, asked permission to introduce a Bill to amend the Act of 1833, but at the request of Lord John Russell the matter was not pressed. Nothing further was done until June 1838 when Ashley again raised the matter, but further action was shelved until July 1839 when it was proposed to grant additional powers to check birth certificates and abolish the right of manufacturers to recover lost time, except in water-powered mills. Ashley opposed the measure unless silk mills were included, and on a division the government was defeated and the Bill withdrawn.

During the next few years the campaign was overshadowed by the Chartist movement, the opposition to the Poor Law Reform of 1834, the Plug Riots of 1842 and the activities of the Anti-Corn Law League. Matters were complicated, as Asa Briggs (39) points out, by the ending of good harvests in 1836 and a trade slump in 1837 with the Liverpool merchants complaining about the distress among the mercantile interests. By the summer of 1838 there were 50,000 unemployed operatives in Manchester, but a revival in trade during 1839 and 1840 was followed by a serious depression in 1842, which involved food riots and strikes; in 1844 Oldham cotton workers went on strike in protest against reduction in wages [doc. 55]. The Plug rioters organised deliberate cessations of work, often accompanied by violence in the Yorkshire and Lancashire towns [doc. 58]. C.P. Hill (91) suggests that these riots were the result of the rejection of the Chartist petition, but there were other factors equally important such as food prices, and the brutal operation of the Poor Law for the temporarily unemployed. The frustration and despair of the factory workers was demonstrated in the destruction of machines and the compulsory stoppage of mills (112).

The Plug Riots began in the Stalybridge and Glossop districts. The operatives at the Glossop mills, as elsewhere, were on strike and to obtain support for their demands were determined to stop all mills in the neighbouring districts. On Friday 12 August 1842 a mob of half-starved operatives moved into Yorkshire via the Colne Valley and Holmfirth. When the crowd demanded that work be suspended at Sykes and Fisher's mill in Marsden and were told to go away, they pulled the wooden plugs out of the boilers, releasing steam and water so bringing the mills to a stop. D.E.F. Sykes (130) gives a vivid description of their activities in Huddersfield, where the mob brought every mill to a halt. The mob which came via the Holme valley visited mills at Sudehill, Scholes, Meltham as well as Lord's Mill in Honley and Cocking Steps at Netherton, stopping all production. Leaving Huddersfield the mob moved towards Wakefield but at Skelmanthorpe they were fed with soup and bread by the sympathetic villagers **(20)**.

A further attempt was made in March 1843 by Sir James Graham to introduce a Bill into the Commons, designed to reduce working hours of children between the ages of nine and thirteen to six and a half hours per day. The hours were to be worked during the morning or afternoon but not divided between the two portions of the day, and at the same time limiting the hours of work on Saturday to nine. It was also proposed to fence dangerous machinery and make education compulsory for all children for three hours each day. There was great opposition to the educational clauses, arising from mere jealousy and hardened attitudes between the Anglican Church and the Nonconformists to religious education for factory workers **(124)**. The Act of 1844 had the educational clauses deleted but created the half-time system for children, giving factory inspectors power to inspect the factory schools, established under previous legislation and to take action to remove incompetent teachers. In January 1846 Ashley made an attempt to introduce another Ten Hours Bill. According to Philip Grant **(80)** petitions poured in from twenty-two Lancashire towns, but unfortunately this projected Bill coincided with the climax to the question of the repeal of the Corn Laws. Following the repeal of the Corn Laws Ashley resigned in protest and left John Fielden to take up the cause of the factory workers, only to see his Bill of 1846 defeated by ten votes.

Ten months later the Tory government was replaced by a Whig administration, and immediately the agitation for a new Ten Hours Bill was revived. In January 1847 such a Bill was introduced **(113)** and a new weekly paper, *The Ten Hours Advocate*, was started in Manchester to support it. The second reading was carried by a majority of 108 votes, the Bill being supported by the leading Whigs, Russell and Grey, with those Tories who had opposed the repeal of the Corn Laws. In May 1847 the Bill became law, but, according to Pauline Gregg **(81)**, a trade depression masked its effect. Nevertheless, according to press reports there were great rejoicings. Manchester, as usual, organised massive celebrations. William Walker of Bradford entertained his 3,000 employees to a feast at Bolling Hall, but for all this children were sent to work at nine years of age in the mills **(145)**.

The first year proved to be satisfactory for the employees, but the employers, especially in the outlying areas, found a way of breaking the law and it was in Lancashire that the largest number of offenders was found. In Glossop the Factory Act was first evaded by working employees in relays or shifts. Complaints were loud and long and factory inspectors took up the matter and brought cases to court. The magistrates gave contradicting sentences which led to discontent. Although the practice of relay working was not in operation in Yorkshire, the conditions under which it was practised in Lancashire and Cheshire made some change in the law essential. David Mills, a manufacturer of Heywood, Lancashire, and a supporter of the Ten Hours campaign, took the case to Parliament. The matter was solved by a further Bill in 1850, when the total working day was restricted to twelve hours and eight on Saturdays, a total of sixty hours a week; this was the only solution acceptable to both sides at the time, although Oastler, Walker and Cobbett opposed it. In the long term the arrangement proved to be acceptable to the majority (23).

A report on cotton mills presented to Parliament in 1849 shows how strenuous and laborious was the craft of mule spinning and also the wide range in the earnings of those concerned. The spinner could earn 50s per week but his piecener only 11s and the scavenger a mere thirty pence (46). Conditions in the mills also varied widely, when the report of the excellent mills of Henry Ashworth of Egerton, for example, is contrasted with that on the horrible disease-ridden mills in Oldham [doc. 60]. The success of the factory reform movement led in turn to legislation controlling the conditions of employment in mines and factories other than cotton or wool.

9 The Church and Factory Reform

A study of this nature would be incomplete if it remained within the bounds of what Dr Margaret Spufford describes as the 'economic' man (128). According to Dr Spufford it is essential for the historian to survey the entire situation and look at the influence of the Church in the sphere of social change. True, the eighteenth-century clergy never for a moment believed the Georgian Church to be an instrument of reform. It was through the movement for the education of the poor by the charity school and Sunday school that Bishop Fisher (1748-1825) became aware, for the first time, of social conditions. Of all the bishops on the Bench only one, Henry Majendie, Bishop of Chester, showed any interest in Peel's Bill of 1802 on the health and morals of apprentices. Majendie urged the clergy to take part in assisting to correct the conditions in the factories which were so injurious to the health of children. Bishop Porteus had realised earlier in 1786 the harmful effects of factory life, after studying a report by Manchester doctors on the outbreak of factory fever in Radcliffe. Having admonished the factory owners, Porteus turned his attention to the abolition of the slave trade (127).

Among petitioners for factory reform in 1818 and 1819 was the Tory George Henry Law, Bishop of Chester, who supported Lords Liverpool, Holland and Kenyon in their efforts to defeat the opposition of Lauderdale to any factory reform, for he wanted the system of free labour to continue. Bishop Law had visited Stockport in 1817 and was horrified when he discovered the conditions in which children were employed (142). In the course of his visitation tour he soon discovered that Stockport was no isolated instance of overworking children. He urged that a committee of enquiry should be set up which brought in long petitions from Lancashire and Cheshire concerning factory conditions. When Lauderdale accused Bishop Law of stirring up agitation, Law countered by more petitions from parents and even from the children themselves (127).

Owen, Peel and Bishop Law wanted all types of factories to be included in the Bill of 1819, but in the end the manufacturing interests obtained the limitation to cotton mills. Law hoped, in vain, that the manufacturers would correct the evil of excessive child labour as a voluntary exercise. What the bishops failed to realise was that spiritual and physical welfare went together and one could not be separated from the other. Whether they liked it or not, churchmen would have to discover, sooner or later, that they would have to concern themselves with the dirty, smelly, disease-ridden bodies of the poor, and before he died Law had realised this.

By 1830 the bishops were less reluctant to discuss social questions, for a new and younger group of bishops were emerging. It was the economic situation that hindered the efforts of the Church to promote spiritual and social contentment. In the sphere of factory reform it was Christian laymen like Oastler, Wood and Fielden who played leading parts. The accusation that factory labour was no concern of the clergy or of the Church brought G.S. Bull, vicar of Bierly, Bradford into the struggle; he became one of the most powerful speakers for factory reform demonstrating that the Church had an interest in social welfare. Criticism of this kind, then as always and even today, comes from the vested interests who dislike reform. When the clergy of Bradford asked permission to visit some factories they were refused entry. Nevertheless Oastler did obtain clerical support for his movement. Richard Oglesby, curate of Woodhouse, Huddersfield, and J.C. Frank, vicar of Huddersfield, spoke at many meetings. J.C. Boddington, curate of Horton, Bradford, was another who corresponded with Oastler on factory reform **(66)**.

G.S. Bull was the driving force for reform, with the support of the rector of Keighley and the vicar of Dewsbury. Dr Fawcett, vicar of Leeds, brought his influence to bear in that parish but he was not the impressive figure that his successor, Dr Hooke, presented. In addition to three vicars in Bradford, support also came from Benjamin Maddock, curate of Holy Trinity, Huddersfield and Sharp of Horbury, all of whom gave strong support to the cause of factory employees. Halifax gave little support to the movement. The curate of Ripponden refused to organise a petition for reform and the vicar of Sowerby believed the clergy should not interfere with business. The nonconformist minister at Coley was angry at the stand made by the Anglican clergy and came out in full support of the manufacturers. The millowners were usually nonconformists themselves and so attacked those clergy who supported reform. Hence the curate of Cragg Vale and the vicar of Hebden Bridge were hated by the manufacturers, who openly referred to the latter as a 'lying priest'.

Generally, in the West Riding textile areas, the local incumbents were on the side of factory reform, with the exception of the Halifax area. In Lancashire they were less active but sympathetic to the movement. The idea that the Church was unsympathetic is taken from a speech made by G.S. Bull in Manchester, where he refers to two ministers out of seventy attending the meetings. Unfortunately Bull lumped together all denominations, including Anglicans, so it is difficult to assess the situation with any accuracy **(78)**. Archbishop Howley's speech on the Rochdale petition was both pointed and direct: that no Christian nation could permit the exploitation of children 'to put money into the pockets of the master manufacturers'. The strong Tory, Archdeacon Pott of London described the manufacturers as, 'seducers, rootless, scribbling, mercenary men' **(73)**. On the whole the bishops who supported reform in 1833 were more often followers than leaders.

Ten years later the picture changed. The bishops showed great interest in the Bill of 1843 and were angry when the hardened nonconformists forced the withdrawal of the education clauses. During the debate of 1847 new bishops such as C.T. Longley of Ripon and Prince-Lee of Manchester, with Wilberforce of Oxford and Blomfield of London spoke out in favour of the Ten Hours Bill. Archbishop Vernon Harcourt of York sent £20 to assist the movement **(79)**.

The Hammonds **(84)** state that the Church was not active in reform before 1840 and imply that support came from the clergy in the small towns, but now there is abundant evidence that it was otherwise. At the same time the Hammonds are correct when they state that the disinterested clergy, especially in Lancashire, came out in favour of reform after 1840. Bull certainly dealt with Christian principles of reform which justified full support in condemnation of the factory system and a wider view of social justice. One influence which churchmen disliked was the growth in the transfer of power to men whose social beliefs carried no sense of responsibility. By this move there was a tendency to undermine the Christian basis of society to the detriment of the community as a whole.

10   The Cotton Famine

No study of the textile industry would be complete without some reference to this event. A great deal has been written upon the subject from the viewpoint of the cotton workers but very little from the employers' side, hence an attempt is being made to redress the balance (147). By 1860 prosperity in the cotton trade encouraged manufacturers to expand their mills and throughout Lancashire and Yorkshire new mills were in course of erection. George Horrocks of Farnworth, writing to his son William in the early part of 1860 referred to the new mills being built around Bolton. Samuel Nuttal had finished his new mill and William Openshaw had begun making bricks and laying the foundation of a mill to hold 8,000 spindles, near Moses Gate station. Nuttal and Long, according to Horrocks, were building what was reputed to be the finest mill in Lancashire. George Horrocks was not behind for he was installing six new throstle frames of 1,200 spindles which commenced to work on 3 December 1860 [doc. 61].

The overall picture was one of abounding prosperity, yet cotton operatives were restless and in Colne, Clitheroe and Blackburn there were strikes (35). In Bolton, weavers demanded an increase of sixpence per cut woven. George Horrocks admitted he had to be as wise as a serpent and bold as a lion to manage his workpeople. The winter of 1860 had been severe and restricted deliveries of raw cotton, but despite these minor problems Horrocks was confident that the demand for cotton would never suffer a decrease so long as children were born naked.

There was serious danger ahead. No one realised how dangerous it was to rely on America as the sole supplier of raw cotton, nor what the effect would be if the source of supply were cut off. Although the American Civil War did not start until April 1861, the price of raw cotton rose steadily. On 3 January 1861 James Garnet of Clitheroe recorded that the quantity of raw cotton available was 400,000 bales less than in the previous year and by May the export of raw cotton to England was reduced by 359,000 bales (25). Horrocks's new throstle frames did not make the expected profit since cotton prices rose far higher than those for the spun yarn. Cotton merchants took advantage of the situation arising from the secession of the Southern States from the Union in the autumn of 1860 when civil war became a possibility, to sell at the highest prices. To the problem of high prices for raw cotton was added the difficulty of selling finished goods in India and China.

The effect of the situation on the employers was a move to reduce their costs and for them the easiest costs to cut were wage rates, so in February 1861 the Blackburn and Clitheroe manufacturers reduced wages by 10 per cent. Strikes followed which, except at Clitheroe where the employees accepted the employers' offer, were settled by arbitration. During the next twelve months the price of cotton increased rapidly from 8*d* per lb in August to 29*d* per lb in September 1861. George Horrocks found the production of cotton cloth with prices for spun yarn at 15*d* per lb, and finished cloth at 14½*d* in 1862 so unprofitable that he closed the mill [doc. 62]; later he reopened it and tried to use Surat cotton but this was far from satisfactory in its results (24).

Other manufacturers turned to short-time working. Thomas Barn worked a seven hour day but others only managed a three day week. At Clitheroe the manufacturers decided to work shorter hours if Dewhurst of Salford Bridge would do the same. The length of the working day did vary with supplies of cotton and in a few instances full time working was possible (84). In the spring of 1862, spinners were seeking cotton from India, Egypt and Peru. The Surat cotton was of a lower quality than American cotton, also dirty and of short fibre so it was impossible to spin finer counts than 40s. Conditions deteriorated rapidly with the manufacturers losing money so heavily that they were compelled to close down. Horrocks refers in his letters to three mills in Darwen and the Co-operative mill losing £120 each week and unable to continue in business (126).

The worst period of the cotton famine was the winter of 1862-63 when many mills entirely closed down. John Ward, the Clitheroe weaver, recorded in his diary, the problems that operatives faced during that winter [doc. 63]. Elizabeth Gaskell in her correspondence alluded to the widespread distress in Manchester and the organisation of relief (106). The Garnet family in Clitheroe organised relief agencies for their own district and subscribed to the relief funds in Manchester. A meeting held on 2 December 1862 under the chairmanship of Lord Sefton raised £130,000 for relief, including a donation of £500 from Lord Derby. The American International Relief Committee of New York organised food supplies for Lancashire. It is by no means a surprise to learn that John Ward concluded his diary for 1864 with the comment, 'nothing but stormy weather and bad work, and a poor prospect for Christmas' **(5)**.

These problems remained unsolved until the events of the first quarter of 1865 in America led to a reduction in the price of raw cotton but it was shortlived. When hostilities terminated on 26 May 1865 there was some return to a more healthy state of affairs in the cotton trade. The demand for yarn and cloth increased rapidly but the supplies of raw cotton only slowly. Not until the close of 1865 were the mills back in full operation, those, that is to say, which had survived the heavy losses incurred through lack of raw materials. Weavers were able to earn 11s.4d per week for two looms, with an average wage in the industry of 13s.3d. Only slowly did the trade recover, and together with woollen textiles maintained their dominant position in the economy until the events of the First World War and its aftermath compelled the whole industry to reorganise and rationalise.

The textile industry is a most complex one in its structure and organisation so it is by no means an easy task to assess the total effect of the introduction of machines and the building of factories on the community as a whole. In the older trade of woollen and worsted fabrics the traditional skills have been utilised and developed, in conjunction with machines, to produce very highly specialised fabrics, often in synthetic materials, and so has been enabled to survive the change in the economy since 1914. The newer industry of cotton textiles forged ahead in the later nineteenth and early twentieth centuries to satisfy the demand for cotton goods on a worldwide scale. As other countries developed their own cotton industry Lancashire has suffered a decline in demand and has had to change to the manufacture of high grade fabrics.

One feature which dominates the landscape in the textile areas is the textile town, with its smoke blackened buildings, its tall mill chimneys, carrying names such as Mons, Kearsley, Bee-Hive, and its massive town halls that speak of Victorian wealth and prosperity. Slum property, that arose as the consequence of the mills, is still to be found but on an increasingly smaller scale. The century of expansion from 1760 to 1860 and beyond has bequeathed to the twentieth century the remnants of militant nonconformity and radical politics in textile communities; in that peculiar creation, the textile town—be it Bolton or Burnley, Batley or Bradford—the same characteristics can still be found. These are well worth the attention of any interested student who desires to undertake a study in depth on this phenomenon for future generations.

PART FOUR

Documents

Agreement to graze sheep

Cistercian abbeys were anxious to increase their wool supplies and often entered into an agreement with a local lord. In this case the Abbot of Byland concluded an agreement with Swain of Bretton.

'Grant in frankalmoin by Swain son of Ulkil de Brettona . . . to God and the monks of St Mary of Byland of all the royd land (cleared land) in the territory of Brettona called Smidroyda and all the land on the West . . . as far as the conduit of Emmelai (Emley) . . . and common pasture for two hundred sheep by the greater Hundred and other beasts . . . throughout all the territory of the said vill; the monks are to make their sheepfold for the said sheep on either side of the said conduit, and to enclose the said land at will. Yielding and paying to the said Swain and his heirs vj shillings yearly.

Yorkshire Deeds, vol. 5 Yorkshire Archaeological Society, 1926.

Ralph Matthews to the Vicar of Leeds, 1588

The vicar of Leeds wrote to Ralph Matthews to ask his opinion about the amount of wool required to keep sixty persons employed in the cloth trade.

Three score persons are thus to be divided; Sorting and dressing 6, Spinning and cardinge 40, Weaving 8, Sheremen 6 whereof 2 may be to help the rest. Two stone being 28lbs. will make 18 yards, yard broade. One stone spinning 2s-4d. Weaving a piece 20d. Walking 3d, Burlinge 2d, Dressing 10d. And 40 spinners will spinne in a week 20 stone. One gallon cyvill oyle (Seville oil) will serve to 4 stone white woolle. The woole about Skiptoun will make no carsies except it be pure white; and at Halifax there is no cloth made but yearde broade carsies. If the stuffe that is bought for lytinge (dyeing) were cheap and easie to be gotten, brode cloth were the best kind of cloth that is to be made about Skiptoun, bycause it is course woolle. Halifax men occupie a fyne woolle most owt of Lincolnshire and their corse wooll they sell to the men of Ratchdeall.

Kenyon MSS, Historical Manuscripts Commission 108-9.

document 3

Defoe's description of the cloth industry

During his tour of England and Wales, Daniel Defoe came to Halifax in 1727. He describes what he found there.

The land near Halifax was divided into small enclosures, from two acres to six or seven each, seldom more. Every three or four pieces of land had an house belonging to them ... hardly an house out of speaking distance from another. ... We could see at every house a tenter and on almost every tenter a piece of cloth, or Kersie or Shalloon. ... At every considerable house was a manufactory. ... Every clothier keeps one horse at least to carry his manufacture to the market; and generally one cow or two, or more, for his family. ... The houses are full of lusty fellows some at the dye vat some at the looms, others dressing the cloths; the women and children carding and spinning, being all employed from the youngest to the oldest. ... Not a beggar or an idle person to be seen.

Daniel Defoe, *Journal of a Tour through England and Wales*, iii, 144.

document 4

Accounts of Thomas Marsden of Bolton 1683

The following is an extract from Marsden's accounts. He was a master clothier who had his yarn spun in the various villages and named the yarn after the place where it was spun.

Delivered 44 pounds of Mellor Weft at 9d p.lb.
    cost   £ 1.13. 0d

Delivered 1187 lb.12 ozs of Mellor Weft at
   5d p.lb.   24.14.11d

For weaving 58 Jeannes No.5 at 2s.6d. per
   end cost   7. 5. 0d

For spinning 290lb Weft at 6d p.lb. put into
   that cloth   7. 5. 0d

For winding 210 doz. Hambarrow Yarn at
   8d per doz. and 12 doz. Quitle barrow Yarn
   at 5d   7. 5. 0d

Quitle barrow, Mellor and Hambarrow are the
   names of hamlets.

A.P. Wadsworth and J. Mann *Cotton Trade and Industrial Lancashire 1660-1780* **(140)**, pp. 83-4.

document 5

Description of hand spinning

The process of manufacturing worsted cloth demanded a high skill in spinning the yarn.

The work was entirely domestic, and its different branches widely scattered over the country. First the manufacturer had to travel on horse back to purchase his raw material amongst the farmers, or at the great fairs. . . . The wool safely received was handed over to the sorters, who rigourously applied the gauge of required length of staple, and mercilessly chopped off by shears or hatchet what did not reach their standards as wool fit only for the clothing trade. The long wool passed into the hands of the combers, and having been brought back by them in the combed state, was again carefully packed and strapped on the back of sturdy horses to be taken into the country and spun. . . . Here at each village, he distributed the wool amongst the peasantry and received it back as yarn. The machine employed was the old, one-thread wheel, and in summer weather . . . might be seen housewives plying their busy trade. Returning with his yarn the manufacturer had to seek out his weavers who ultimately delivered to him his fabric ready for sale to the merchant or delivery to the dyer.

W. James, *History of the Worsted Manufacture* **(97)** p. 323.

Problems in dyeing Turkey Red

Although John Wilson attempted to dye cotton fabrics by using Turkish methods, he was unsuccessful until yarn could be spun by the new machines.

In the year 1753, I sent a young Man to Turkey, on purpose to learn to dye it. He had lived with a Mr Richard Dobs, a merchant in Smyrna, some Time before, and had learned the Language of those Greeks who dye it; and by Mr Dob's interest, got admittance into their Dye-houses, and was instructed; and on his Return, brought the true Method, and with him a many Bales of the best Madder Root, pronounced by them Choke Biaugh; and a letter from Mr Dobs, to assure me he would buy for me every Thing I might Want, on a very moderate Commission. . . . when I had got it, to my great Disappointment it would not suit my purpose, that is for Cotton Velvets; nor any other sort of Piece Work I then made. The Tediousness of so many Operations, and the Exactness required, every Time rendered it of no more value to me than Madder red . . . which is so easily dyed, whereas the Turkey Red requires 12 or 13 Operations in repeated Steepings, Dryings, Washings and Dyeing . . . At the time I procured it, all Cotton Yarn was spun with a single Spindle from Rovings, carded the transverse or cross-way of the harle or filaments of the Cotton, which made it liable to chase, and be ruffled by so many Operations in wetting, drying etc.

Wadsworth and Mann (140) p. 180.

Slaithwaite fulling mills 1678-1684

These mills were owned by the Earl of Dartmouth and the accounts reveal some of the problems in operating fulling mills.

1678. The two Fulling Milnes milned this half yeare 1740 peices which att 6d a peice comes to £43.2.0d butt Strangers for their encouragement hath usually something returned.

The Milners wages this half yeare came to £28.8s.4d of which £23 of itt was for the new house at the lower miln and a new wheel making so that the remainder of this half yeare came butt to £6.15s.9d.

1684 The two Fulling Milns milned this half yeare (notwithstanding the long and great want of water thorow the longest Frost and Droughtyest summer that was ever heard of) 1435 peices, 271 of them was Strangers out of the Manor or Lordship of Slaighwaite and these payes but 5d a peice, if they have six or above uppon account. The remainder are 1164 which are all made within this Lordshipp and these pay 6d for every peice. The Milners wages (they have five farthings for every peice milned) amounts this half yeare to £7.13s.7d given to each of them and other disbursements about the Milns and Damms to £4.6s.4d soe that this halfe yeare clear profitt if all be gott will amount to att the rates abovesaid £22.15s.

Earl of Dartmouth, Rental Book 1678-1688, Leeds City Archives.

document 8

Penistone Cloth Hall 1743

The Penistone clothiers agreed to eastablish a cloth market at Penistone instead of Sheffield and the fullers agreed not to full cloth for any non-member. Ninety-one clothiers signed of whom twenty-two were unable to write their names.

Whereas All or the Greatest Part of the Clothmakers in and about the parish of Penistone have sometimes lately brought their Cloth to Penistone to Sell and having had good Encouragement therein by the Mercers for the Sale of their Cloth and the Greatest Part of the Trades people (the Clothiers in that Neighbourhood deal with) being desirous that there may be a Meeting at Penistone Established, And we whose hands and Seals are hereunto sett having agreed to bring our Cloth to Penistone instead of carrying the same to Sheffield for the better encouragement of the Woollen Manufacture in the West Riding of the County of York. . . . . Know all persons by these presents, . . . we . . . Covenant, promise, Grant and agree to and with Aymor Rich of Bullhouse in the parish of Peniston... gentleman and George Walker of Hunshelf... that such of us as shall directly or indirectly Sell, expose for Sale by ourselves, Servants or Agents any Kersey cloth or plaines... at Sheffield... shall well and truly upon demand pay unto the said Aymor Rich and George Walker the sum of Three Pounds for every peice of cloth that such persons shall... expose for Sale at Sheffield. 10 November 1743.

Marquis of Crewe muniments, CM969, CM970, Sheffield City Archives.

document 9

Proctors' trade papers 1633-1634

These attestations by several merchants show the kind of trade in cloth. In this case the cargo ship, 'Susan of Hull' had been captured by a privateer Peter Willert and taken to Ostend.

I Thomas Metcalfe of the town of Leeds in England, merchant attest that I shipped 121 parcells of cloth called Dozens and 45 parcells of Carsies sealed and numbered in the margin. Consigned to my factor Bernardo Hermanson in Amsterdam.

I Henry Watkinson of the town of Leeds merchant attest that I consigned six parcells called Short Clothes and 19 parcells called Single Dozens to Bernado Hermanson in Amsterdam.

I John Thompson of the City of York merchants attest that I consigned in the 'Merchant of Hull' 25 parcells of cloth called Dozens and 8 parcells of cloth called Kerseys worth £140 of English money to the City of Hamburg in Germany. *The ship was lost after a collision with the 'Endeavour' in the North Sea.*

Proctors' Trade Papers, Borthwick Institute of Historical Research,

Life in Netherton 1860

The embryo of the modern mill is to be observed in the organisation described by Tom Dyson.

All the folks in the district were hand loom weavers, and Tom Dyson, father of George Dyson, manufactured cloth. He had the yarn spun at Marsden and they used to come once a week into the Square; skeps of Yarn came on carts drawn by mules. All the weavers on the Square worked for Dyson. He compelled every family to take care of their urine to scour pieces and there used to be a large tub at the top of the stairs in every chamber. . . . Old Eli fetched the urine in a four wheeled barrel. The hand loom weavers earned twenty or thirty shilling a week.

J. Oldfield, *Recollections of Netherton,* 1910.

Inventory of Richard Wright of Leeds 1684

Inventories always include details of the tools of the deceased man's trade as well as his household goods.

	£	s	d
Imprimis his purse and Cloths	1	10	0
Item in the Great Parlour one standing bed one stockbed one Fetherbed and two Flockbeds with all the furniture belonging to them	5	0	0
Item one Cubberd, one pewter doubler, two standing Quision	1	1	0
Item one tabel and a forme		6	0
Item one Truncke 3 Chests one Coffer two great Stooles			
Two Cussions one seeing glass	1	10	0
In the Little Parlour. one Fall bed with furniture, 3 doublers, one Chamber Pott one pewter can	1	0	0

In the House, one range, 3 brass potts, 5 panns one Brass morter 3 spits, one paire of Tongs, one fire shovel	3	0	0
Item one warming pan, 2 Candelsticks, 6 flagons, 16 quarts 3 Cups, 6 salt sellers	3	0	0
For Lyne and Yarn		11	0
In the Working Shop. 9 paire of Shears; one press with all things belonging to it; 2 Sheare Boards, Trussles, 2 foot Boards, 14 lead Weights, 2 sett Brushes, 3 stoning boards 2 Scarges, 2 stone of Tassels (teazles) one burling board	10	0	0
One Bruing of Drincke		12	0
Debts owing to the deceased	80	0	0

Kirkgate Wills, Leeds, DB/147/1, Leeds City Archives.

document 12

A clothier's diary 1782-84

These extracts are designed to show the variety of the life of a West Riding clothier. Note the high death rate in 1782.

1782 November 1. A fine frosty clear droughty day. Sized a warp and Churned in the forenoon. In the afternoon wove five yards.

December 29 I went to Halifax, heard Mr Knight preach. I saw 10 open graves in Halifax churchyard, 9 of them for Children & was informed that 110 Children had been interred in the Graveyard in 4 weeks which died of smallpox.

1783 August 16. I churned, sized a warp in the morning. Went to Halifax and saw Two men hanged on Becon Hill sentenced at York for activity in Riot.

1784 January 7. Christmas Holiday being over I wove five yards. Ben Blagborough at Illingworth buried his son Thomas.

January 18. A fine frosty day. I was employed in Preparing a Calf Stall & Fetching the Tops of three Plain Trees home which grew in the Lane and was that day cut down & sold to John Blagborough.

July 3 I went into Wheaty & made Rope Shades & other jobbs. got my warp died and siz'd it again & Loom'd part of it.

July 11 employ'd in filling up Part of the damm & other work. Went to Halifax and bought a New Hat at 12/-.

Had a new wheelbarrow brought home.

Apprentice indenture 1778

This is an extract from the lengthy indenture by which all apprentices to a trade were bound. The conditions vary according to the terms of the charity under which the apprentice was bound.

THIS INDENTURE WITNESSETH that James son of Jane Walton widow of Kirkham in the County of Lancaster by his own free will and with the Consent Approbation, Appointment and Direction of the Trustees for the Charity of the Reverend James Barker, Clerk, deceased for putting out Poor Children Apprentice and belonging to the said Township of Kirkham, Hath put, bound and placed James Walton unto Richard Hornby of Kirkham, Taylor . . . unto the full end and Term of Seven years . . . [he] doth covenant and agree to teach and Instruct . . . the said Apprentice in the Trade, Art, Mistery or Occupation of a Taylor . . . shall also find and provide the said Apprentice with sufficient Meat, Drink, Washing and Lodging, Together with suitable Apparrel of all sorts and shall allow the said Apprentice two weeks in the Writing month to Learn to Write on Accounts yearly during said Term, and at the end of the said Term shall turn out the said Apprentice in sufficient clothing suitable to his degree.

A household under the domestic system

Samuel Bamford, a contemporary of the late eighteenth century, has left a diary and several eyewitness records of Lancashire life, amongst them this description of a typical family.

Farms were then mostly cultivated for the production of milk, butter and cheese. Oats for the family's consumption of meal in the form of porridge and oaten cakes, would be looked after; and a small patch of potatoes, when they had come into general use, would probably be found on some favourable bank attached to each farm. The farming was generally of the kind which was soonest and most easily performed, and it was done by the husband and other males of the family, whilst the wives and daughters and maid servants, if there were any of the latter, attended to churning, cheesemaking, carding slubbing and spinning of wool or cotton as well as forming it into warps for the loom. The husband and sons would next, at times when the farm labour did not call them abroad, size the warp, dry it and beam it in the loom, and either they or the females . . . would weave the warp down. . . . If the rent was raised from the farm so much the better; if not the deficiencies were made up from the manufacturing profits.

S. Bamford, *Dialect of South Lancashire* (32), p.4.

Problems in selling cloth 1739-1740

These two letters from John Firth illustrate the problems of receiving enough cash from sales to buy raw materials and of transport in winter.

1 June 1739   To Messrs Lord & Wolfinden
Sirs,
    I duly received yours with advice that the 25 Shalloons & 60 Long Ells were come safe to Hand & if they are not already sold, I desire you to sell them as soon as possible, & as I said in my last for quick payment as you can. For

Midsummer Time drawing nigh when all the Makers want their Money to buy their wool with, makes me more desirous to hear they are sold I leave the Price to you & the Chance of a good Market & when you have disposed of these shall send you more.

John Firth.
Robert Rodgers.

2 Feb. 1739/40   Robert Rodgers.
I duly received yours and observe you expect to want 50 pieces I.B.F. with which I shall be glad to serve you by Land Carriage for I take it that no vessells dare go down the River from Leeds for the great pieces of Ice that will be brought down by the Torrent 'till 3 weeks after the frost breaks, besides there are large lumps of Ice floating in the Humber . . .

John Firth's Letter Book, 1739/40, HAS 321, Halifax Central Library

document 16

John Kay's petition for assistance

John Kay, in this crudely spelled letter, asks for some reward for his invention from the government.

As you cannot find out no wea to gratifie mee for what I have shoad you that will be of ane sarvis to mee for that reason I will not sho you ane more, in fore or five months time, I could meack your shuttle meackers and weavers parfect so that they might do as well without me as with me, my resolucion is this that except you can find sum wea to ease me ten or twelve thousand pound of the factres that my invenchens will be of sarvis to to be pead mee in five years time at fore or five set times without that i will not meack ane bargain with you at all.

Wadsworth and Mann (140), p. 459.

Report on the fly shuttle 1760-63

The new shuttle aroused some opposition but some weavers found they could profit by using this and so installed fly shuttles secretly.

Mr John Kay . . . having set several of the Wheel Shuttles to work on broad Woollen Goods, it appeared that one Man would do as much Work, and better with the Wheel Shuttle as two Men with the Hand Shuttle, upon which the Weavers concluded that in Consequence . . . one half the Weavers then employed in the broad Woollen way must (if the Wheel Shuttle went forward) starve for want of Employment. The Weavers therefore assembled in a Mob, determined to hinder the Wheel Shuttles Progress by killing of Mr John Kay, the Inventor who very narrowly escaped by flight; the Mob went to the Houses where some of the Wheel Shuttles were at work and forcibly seized and burned them, and otherwise ill-used the Houses, yet notwithstanding the Threats of the Mob etc. several Manufacturers who lived at a Distance from the Places where the Mobs assembled being sensible of the Benefit which would arise to them, if they could Manufacture their Goods upon easier Terms than their Neighbours, got the Wheel Shuttles fixed upon Looms in their own Houses; the Weavers for the most part, did all in their Power (by loitering away their Time and spoiling their work) to keep their Masters ignorant of the Advantages which attended Wheel Shuttles.

H.T. Wood, Invention of John Kay, *Journal of the Society of Arts,* LX.

Report on Spinning Jennies

At first the jenny was considered to be an invention leading to unemployment but the magistrates tried to convince spinners such a machine was in their interests.

What rioting was there in this County . . . upon the invention of the Spinning Jennies. Many people foreboded the most dreadful consequence from them. The common cry was, that they would take the bread from the Poor, and throw them out of employment. Upon this a mob arose, burnt what Machines they could find and carried the fragments about in triumph. The persons who did this thought they were doing a service to the country by destroying those terrible engines which were about to impoverish and ruin the land. . . . Dorning Ramsbotham a worthy magistrate convinced the weavers . . . that it was their true interest to encourage jennies . . . for the demand for twist for warps was greater as weft grew plenty, therefore engines were soon constructed for this purpose.

Wadsworth and J Mann, *Thoughts on the Use of Machines in Cotton Manufacture*, pp. 478-9

document 19

Problems concerning the quality of yarn

The inability of the single thread wheel to produce yarn of even twist caused problems in weaving even cloths.

Whenever a Clothier has Occasion for a Parcel of Yarn to be spun to any particular Degree of Size or Twist he is obliged to have a much greater Quantity spun than he wants . . . in order that among the whole he may pick out as much as will answer his then Occasion, By means whereof the Remainder often becomes a dead Stock upon his hands for a considerable Time and . . . the poorer Part of the Clothiers are frequently rendered incapable of serving their Customers from an Inability to keep a large Stock of the various Sizes and Sorts of Yarn by them, and often . . . they are obliged to use such sorts of Yarn as they have by them or they can get tho' of different Sizes and Degrees of Twist which occasions the said Goods to be unsuitable.

State Papers Domestic, Petition Book 254 f.466, PRO.

Letter from Samuel Crompton on his Mule 1802

Crompton gave details of his experiments to improve spinning to a Commission on the Textile Industry in 1802.

According to your request [I] have Applied to Several Gentle[men] in this neighbourhood who were personally concerned & Subscribers to the machine or Spinning Wheels which I had made. I then lived at a place called Hall-oth-Wood and they went by that name here-with you they have the name of Mule.

About the year 1772 I Began to Endeavour to find if possible a better Method of making Cotton Yarn than was then in Generall Use, being grieved at the bad yarn I had to Weave. But to be short, it took me Six Years, that is till the year 1778, before I could make up my mind what plan to Adopt that would be equal to the task I hoped it would perform. It took from 1778-1779 to finish it. From 1779 to the beginning of 1780 I spun upon it for my own use, both warp and weft. In the beginning of the year 1780 I Began to Spin only and left off Weaving.

G.W. Daniels, *Early English Cotton Industry* (57), p. 166-7.

Carding machine for sale, 1779

This is the earliest known sale advertisement in the press offering a carding machine for sale.

TO BE SOLD. A complete Scribbling-machine with new Rollers, carrying 46 Pairs of Cards with Iron-geer in good Condition; together with an upright Shaft, Swimming Wheel and Nutt (capable to carry 4 machines) with Tumbling Shaft and Nutt. Also a smaller Machine of seven Barrels or Rollers with cards in good Condition. Likewise a Teazing Mill on a new construction with the GEER thereunto belonging, to go by water. Particulars may be had by applying to J. Kenworthy of Huddersfield the owner.

Leeds Mercury, 26 January 1779.

Petition to halt introduction of machines 1786

Leeds clothiers were concerned lest the spread of machines should lead to unemployment and poverty on a vast scale.

That the Scribbling-Machines have thrown thousands of your petitioners out of employ, whereby they are brought into great distress and are not able to procure a maintainance for their families, and deprive them of the opportunity of bringing up their children to labour; We have therefore to request that prejudice and self-interest may be laid aside and that you may pay that attention to the following facts which the nature of the case requires. The number of Scribbling-Machines extending about seventeen miles south-west of LEEDS exceed all belief being no less than ONE HUNDRED AND SEVENTY and as each machine will do as much work in twelve hours as ten men can do in that time by hand ... and they working night and day, one machine will do as much work in one day as would employ twenty men.

... upon a moderate computation twelve men are thrown out of employment for every single machine used in scribbling; and as it may be supposed the number of machines in all other quarters together nearly equal those in the South-West, full four thousand men are left to shift for a living how they can and must fall on the Parish if not timely relieved. Allowing one boy to be bound apprentice from each unemployed family, eight thousand hands are deprived of the opportunity of getting a livelihood. We therefore hope that the feelings of humanity will lead those who have it in their power, to prevent the use of these machines ... so prejudicial to their fellow creatures.

Leeds Mercury, 13 June 1786.

Visitation return from Bolton, 1778

In 1778, Beilby Porteus, Bishop of Chester, held his primary visitation. One of the questions he asked concerned the size of the parish and its industry. The vicar of Bolton replied to the questions.

The Parish of Bolton is from its Southern to its Northern
Extremity twenty miles in Extent from East to West, its
Breadth is considerable but frequently intermixed on the
S.W. Side with the Parishes of Middleton Dean, and Standish.
It contains . . . 16 Townships . . . Bolton being the center of
the Cotton Manufacture is extremely populous, but too near
Manchester which is the great Mart, to have many opulent
Tradesmen resident in it— the Number of Houses in Bolton
are about 1500 and in the rest of the Parish not less than
9000, three-fourths of which are Cottages inhabited by
Weavers and other labouring Poor. In different parts of the
Parish are many old deserted Mansions formerly the Resi-
dences of families of some Note. At present James Bradshaw
Esq. of Darcy Lever and Robert Andrews of Rivington, two
Gentlemen in the Commission of the Peace are its principal
Inhabitants.

Articles Preparatory to Visitation 1778, EDV7/1/83, Cheshire Record
Office.

document 24

Building and equipping a mill, 1784

*To erect and equip a mill was no light undertaking, for capital sums
well over £2,000 were required.*

An Estimate of the cost of a Building to be 52 feet long and
31 feet Wide from outside to outside, 1½ Brick thick Walls,
to be 50 feet high, to have 35 windows and 35 Backwards
opposite each other for the purpose of Carding Roving
Spinning Cotton to be erected on Henry Ashcroft's Farm in
Eccleston near to the Brook side opposite an Estate in Windle
called Tanhouse.

Building and conveyance of water only	£993; 0; 0
24 Spinning Frames at £25 each	600; 0; 0
5 Carding Engines at £20 each	100; 0; 0
2 Tumbling Engines at £20 each	40; 0; 0
3 Roving Frames at £20 each	60; 0; 0
2 Drawing Frames at £10 each	20; 0; 0

Sundry utensils for carrying on the work	50; 0; 0
Agents wages, sundry expenses	70; 0; 0
Cost of cutting water channels, banks, and dam	223; 3; 0

Scarisbrick Papers, DDSc. 12/135, Lancashire Record Office.

document 25

Agreement on water rights 1819

The building of a mill at Walsden, Todmorden meant protection of water rights in Ramsden Clough and protection of rights of way.

Memorandum . . . between John Foster of Slack in the Township of Heptonstall in the Parish of Halifax . . . and Clement Hall of Rochdale on behalf of John Entwistle of Foxholes in Rochdale . . . the said John Foster is owner of the Strines Estates and the said John Entwistle is owner of the Ramsden Estate—the said John Foster agrees that the said John Entwistle shall enjoy all the water running down a certain Clough called Ramsden Clough so far downward as the highest extremity of the Top Goit of Strines Mill and so far upward as the said Strines Estate adjoins the Ramsden Estate . . . the said John Entwistle to cause the Water descending from a Mill hereafter to be built by them . . . to run and flow into the Top Goit of Strines Mill at the place where the Water is taken out of Strines Clough at present . . . John Entwistle agrees to grant to the said John Foster right of way and passage upon his private road leading from the Halifax, Burnley and Littleborough Turnpike road at or near the Walsden Turnpike Gate to his Ramsden Estate . . . leading over Strines Clough to Strines Mill the said John Foster being at one fourth of the Expenses to the repairs of the said Road.

Sutcliffe Papers 133, Leeds City Archives.

document 26

Sentence passed on rioters, 1780

The magistrates dealt severely with the rioters who destroyed Arkwright's mill at Birkacre near Chorley as a demonstration of their hatred of machines.

Whereas Mary Leicester otherwise Lister otherwise Knight appearing in Court in the Custody of the Governor of the House of Correction at Preston ... having been Indicted, Tried and Convicted at this Session of a misdeameanour for that she with several other persons to the number of Twenty and more at Birkacre within Chorley ... Entered the Mill ... Unlawfully, Riotously and attacked and Broke, Burned and Destroyed twenty Engines ... called Spinning Engines, Twenty ... called Twisting Engines, Twenty Cotton Wheels and Twenty Cotton Reels ... the property of Richard Arkwright, Jedidiah Strutt ... This court doth ... committ her ... to His Majesty's Gaol the Castle of Lancaster in safe custody for the term of Twelve Months Absolutely and from the Expiration of that Term for a further Term of Six Months, Unless she enter into a recognizance ... in the manner following ... the said Mary Leicester in the sum of £100 and two Suretes in £50 each.

Quarter Sessions Orders, 1780, Lancashire Record Office.

document 27

Resolution of Quarter Sessions 1779

Lancashire Quarter Sessions for the summer of 1779 confirmed that it would support the introduction of machines as beneficial and not injurious.

RESOLVED that it is the Unanimous Opinion of the Court that the Sole Cause of the Riots, Tumults, and Insurrections that have lately happened in the County of Lancaster is owing to the Erection of Certain Mills and Engines within the said County, for the manufacture of Cotton which in the idea of Persons Assembled tend to Depreciate the price of Labour. RESOLVED unanimously that it is the Opinion of this Court after the Examination of many Witnesses that the Invention and Introduction of the Machines for Carding, Roving, Spinning and Twisting Cotton has been of the greatest Utility to this Country by the extension and improvement of the Cotton Manufacturers and affording Labour and Subsistence to the Industrious Poor, who have not had any pretence for Committing the late Riots from want of work.

RESOLVED ... that it is impossible to Restrain the force of Ingenuity in the Improvement of Manufactures ... That the destroying of Machines in one County only Serves to prevent the Exercise of them in this Kingdom, it would tend to Establish them in Foreign Countreys which would be highly Detrimental to the Trade of this County.

Quarter Sessions Orders, 1779, Lancashire Record Office.

document 28

Sale of a mill, 1793

From time to time the press began to advertise not only machines but entire mills for sale.

TO BE SOLD by private Contract. Situate near Balm Beck in Hunslet in the Parish of Leeds. All that Scribbling Mill consisting of Five Machines and a Willey turned by a Fire Engine also a Scribbling Machine and a Carding Machine turned by a Beck or Rivulet called Balm Beck together with two Billeys. Thomas Rainforth of Hunslet will show the premises.

Leeds Intelligencer, 28 October 1793.

document 29

Armley fulling mills 1790

Leeds clothiers express their gratitude for the opening of two fulling mills which will reduce their travelling time.

We the Trustees of the Mixed Cloth Hall in the Town of Leeds, fully sensible of the great Advantage likely to arise to the Manufacturers of Broad Woollen Cloths by the very compleat manner in which the Fulling Mills in Armley are now finished, think it our Duty to return thanks to Thomas Lloyd Esquire for the great expense he has incurred in the erection of so arduous and undertaking and for the accomodation of his Fulling Mills which will render a part of the Manufacturing Country hitherto much distressed for the want of such covenience that the Clothiers in a dry season were often compelled to go eight or ten miles and sometimes even more to get their Cloth milled. We also sincerely hope that our Brethren the Clothiers will give every encouragement in their power to the above Mills that the owner may receive such reimbursements as his public spirit deserves for the completion of so patriotic so praiseworthy an undertaking.

Leeds Mercury, 12 January 1790.

document 30

Parish apprentices

Samuel Romilly describes the fate of pauper apprentices sent to the cotton mills.

It is a very common practice with the great populous parishes in London to bind children in large numbers to the proprietors of the cotton-mills in Lancashire and Yorkshire, at a distance of 200 miles. The children, who are sent off by wagon loads at a time, are as much lost for ever to their parents as if they were shipped off for the West Indies. The parishes that bind them, by procuring a settlement for the children at the end of forty days, get rid of them for ever; and the poor children have not a human being in the world to whom they can look up for redress of wrongs they may be exposed to. . . . Instances have recently occurred of masters, who, with 200 apprentices have become bankrupts and been obliged to send their apprentices to the poorhouse of the parish in which their mill happens to be, to be supported by strangers who consider them as fraudulently thrown on them for relief.

S. Romilly, *Life of Samuel Romilly,* II, 188.

document 31

Resolution on parish apprentices 1784

On discovering that parish apprentices were being employed on night work, the Lancashire magistrates passed the following resolution.

RESOLVED That is is the Opinion of this Court that it is highly expedient for the Magistrates in this County to Refuse their Allowance to all Indentures of parish Apprentices who shall be Bound to the Owners of Cotton Mills or other Manufactories in which Children are obliged to Work in the Night or more than Ten Hours in a Day.

And it is Ordered that this Resolution shall be Communicated to the Clerks of the Peace for the Counties of Chester, Stafford, Flint, Denbigh, Derby, York and Westmorland and that the same shall be published in the Manchester Newspapers.

Quarter Sessions Orders, 1784, Lancashire Record Office.

document 32

Resolution to limit apprentices, 1781

The resolution passed at a meeting of Oldham weavers to prevent the dilution of the trade.

Whereas an evil and pernicious custom has of late prevailed among the linen and cotton weavers in the parish of Oldham by introducing a number of unfair and illegal hands into that branch of the trade; This is to give Notice, that we, the said Weavers . . . within the parish of Oldham are resolved and do intend to put a stop to so vile a practice and we do declare that no person from and after 19 October 1781, who does not serve a legal apprenticeship as the act passed in the fifth year of the Reign of Queen Elizabeth directs, will not be considered, nor treated as a member of the trade. And we further declare that no person who hath more than two apprentices at one time (exclusive of his own children) agreeable to the same act, will not be deemed a fair member thereof-hereby cautioning all parents and others not to place or bind their children to any person who hath more apprentices than as specified above, as they will not when their time is expired be deemed a legal member of the trade.

J. Boardman, *Cotton Spinning in Oldham* 1971

Weavers' demonstrations, 1781

The reaction of the magistrates to demonstrations by weavers for the enforcing of the apprenticeship regulations.

WHEREAS there have been numerous meetings of weavers . . . in Manchester, Oldham etc, under the pretence of regulating trade and the prices of labour which said meetings may be of dangerous consequences to the people who attend them and the country in general. We do . . . most earnestly exhort and advise all such weavers and others quietly and peaceably to demean themselves to avoid unlawful Combination and tumultuous meetings and do signify our intended and determined purpose to prevent all riots and tumults. We do hereby give this notice; That in case we shall be necessitated to read the Riot Act, we will at the time of such reading, cause a BLUE FLAG to be displayed and if the mobs shall not within one hour after . . . disperse themselves in peace or shall commit any act of violence . . . we shall cause a RED FLAG to be displayed to denote that force will be used to disperse them.

Quarter Sessions Orders, September 1781, Lancashire Record Office.

Petition of Preston weavers 1813

Earnings of hand loom weavers had fallen so low that the weavers ask the magistrates to regulate wages under the Act of 1563 and 1603.

SHEWETH that the wages earned by your Petitioners for two years last past have upon average been after the rate of from nine shillings to twelve shillings per Cut for the 120 Reed Cambric amounting in the whole to about twelve shillings per week for a good Workman out of which may be deducted;

For shop room and Brushes	7d week
Materials for dressing warps	8d week
Winding	1s 3d week
Candles in winter time	6d week
	3s 0d week

The above statement does not include Looming ware etc . . . the weekly sum of nine shillings per ann. . . . would in time of Great Plenty be but a scanty Provision but at this time when every Article of Life and more especially those of Provision most in use as Food amongst persons of our description is increased to a price enormous beyond all former examples is a very inadequate means of support for a large family . . . the workman is compelled to labour from fourteen to sixteen hours in the day and not infrequently thro' the night and for want of the necessaries of life and being unable to follow any other calling . . . many of the Families of your Petitioners are at this moment reduced to the most abject state of Poverty, Disease and Misery.

. . . at a time when other parts of this and some neighbouring counties have been disgraced by riots and other offences to subvert all order, the Peace of the District in which your Petitioners reside has remained tranquil and undisturbed.

Quarter Sessions Petitions, January 1813, Lancashire Record Office.

document 35

Conditions of hand loom weavers 1826

Joseph Lawson outlines some of the problems facing hand loom weavers.

It was quite common even when trade was bad to see weavers and spinners going from place to place seeking work, or to get a piece of cloth to make. If they succeeded it was mostly on condition that they helped to break the wool for it; that is opened the bales, then the fleeces, taking off the coarse parts . . . put it in sheets, then go to the mill, help to scour it, then lit or dye it and the morning after take it out of the dye pans into sheets ready for the dryhouse . . . All this was done for nothing except in some cases a small allowance for a little ale or cheese and bread. However after doing all this work the weaver did feel somewhat relieved knowing that he had a claim now to a share in working it up when he could get a set of clubs to be spinning on the jenny.

J. Lawson, *Progress in Pudsey,* 1866.

The cotton mill 1821

A Manchester cotton spinner composed the following eulogy in praise of cotton mills.

> Now see the Cotton from the town convey'd
> To Manchester, that glorious mart of trade;
> Hail splendid scene; the Nurse of every art
> That glads the widow's and the orphan's heart.
> Thy Mills, like gorgeous palaces, arise
> And lift their useful turrets to the skies.
> See Kennedy's stupendous structure joined
> To thine McConnell-friends of human kind
> Whose ready doors for ever wide expand
> To give employment to a numerous band.
> Murray's behold; that well deserves a name
> And Lee and Houldsworth our attention claim
> And numerous others, scattered up and down
> The sole supporters of this ample town.

John Jones, *The Cotton Mills*, 1821.

Weaver's folk song

This type of folk song evolved during the Industrial Revolution as a means of expressing their problems and poverty.

> Poverty, poverty knock
> Me loom is a-saying all day.
> Poverty, poverty knock.
> The Gaffer's too skinny to pay.
> Poverty, poverty knock,
> Keeping one eye on the clock.
> Ah know ah can guttle
> When ah hear me shuttle
> Go: Poverty, poverty knock
>
> Up every morning at five.
> Ah wonder that we keep alive.
> Tired and yawnin' on the cold mornin',
> It's back to the dreary old drive.

We've got to wet our own yarn,
By dippin' it into the tarn.
It's wet and soggy and makes us feel groggy,
An' there's mice in that dirty old barn.

Sometimes a shuttle flies out,
Gives some poor woman a clout.
There she lies bleedin', but nobody's heedin'
Who's goin' to carry her out.

Tuner should tackle me loom.
'E'd rather sit on his bum.
'E's far too busy a-courtin' our Lizzie,
Ah cannot get him to come.

Lloyd, *Folk Song in England*, collected by A.E. Green, 1967, pp. 328-30.

document 38

Bolton in 1890

This description of Bolton should be contrasted with that of 1778 to see how the industrial changes had affected the town.

Looking south, we can count nearly 200 tall chimneys, rising ugly over a mass of brick buildings, that look as if they had stood for years in a climate where it rained ink every day. In addition to 152 cotton spinning firms there are 17 engineering firms . . . about 20,000 houses of every sort from slum hovel to the outskirt villa, . . . and 75 places of worship in all (one to about every 1,500 inhabitants) 520 hotels and beer houses, 200 butchers, 35 pawnshops, 170 confectioners, 127 greengrocers, 30 tripe dealers, 85 cloggers . . . 80 doctors . . . 560 provision dealers, 1 theatre, 2 music halls . . . You will note there are more soul-savers than body physicians; and while there are 520 beerhouses there are only 60 elementary schools . . .

Broadly the population of this town can be divided into three castes and we may begin this classification in the cemetery where it ends. There are three sorts of graves as there are three styles of railway carriages; first-class, second-class and third-class; and probably on the resurrection morn, the first-class corpses will have the privilege of being first to be raised. The first caste . . . dwell in the wide suburban streets, inhabiting villas, semi-detached and single, shopping at the big stores, drinking in the grand hotels, occupying the front cushioned seats near the pulpit in church or chapel . . . having pictures, book-cases, wine-cellars and often private carriages.

The second caste lives in narrower streets . . . drink their beer at smaller hotels, buy food and clothes at the smaller stores (maybe the Co-op) use the middle and near pews in church, get books from the public library, walk or use the tram.

The third caste . . . live in small houses joined together to save space in the narrow streets; they shop at the smallest and dirtiest shops, they drink in low taverns, they get their music in hideous singing rooms, they have no books, no church . . . no art.

A. Clarke, *The Effects of the Factory System* (**54**).

document 39

A cotton spinner's budget, 1835

The weekly earning were twenty-five shillings and 75 per cent of the wages were spent on necessaries.

1½ lbs. butter	1s. 3d
1½ ozs. tea	4½d
Bread baked at home	4s. 6d
½ peck oatmeal	6½d
1½ lbs. bacon	9d
40 lbs. potatoes	1s. 4d
7 quarts milk	1s. 9d
1 lb. meat on Sunday	7d
1½ lb. sugar	9d
Pepper salt etc	3d
Soap and candles	1s. 0d
Coals	1s. 6d
Rent	3s. 6d
Total	18s. 1d

Balance remaining for education, clothes, sickness etc 6s.11d.

Factory Inquiry Commission 1st Report, Section D, 1833.

document 40

Sale of a mill in Halifax, 1804

As the Napoleonic War continued, notices of this type appeared in the press as mills became bankrupt.

HEBBLE MILL near HALIFAX.   To be sold by Auction in lots by Order of the Assignees of Messrs John & Samuel Lees, Bankrupts . . . at the House of Mr John Wright, the Old Cock Inn in Halifax.

The HEBBLE MILL in Wheatley near Halifax being three Stories high containing three Rooms each 86ft long and 32ft wide, and three other Rooms each 50ft long, one of them 24ft wide and the other two 36ft wide, each with Drums (pulleys) for Machinery turned by a Water Wheel 24ft in diameter and 6ft wide and a Crank Steam Engine, Cylinder 42ins in Diameter with two large Boilers. The Water Wheel is supplied by the Hebble Brook and a spacious Dam, the Fall of Water 24ft. A Warehouse adjoining 134ft by 24ft and 4 Storeys high with a Smith's Shop at the end of it. A dyehouse 210ft long and 18ft wide and at the end of it a Building 2 Storeys high 20ft by 18ft.

Leeds Intelligencer, 13 August 1804.

document 41

Rumour concerning riots 1812

Widely conflicting rumours were circulating as to the real cause of the Luddite riots. John Howson, writing to John Spencer, reports what he thinks is the cause.

Mr Radcliffe [a manufacturer] of Mills Bridge [Huddersfield] has received a letter. I understand it is thought that the

Roman Catholics are at the Head of this dreadful business-several suspicious People have been seen (in the daytime) lurking about the Neighbourhood. This Morning Mr West has been alarmed by a person going into his house at Rawroyd . . . he sent in great haste for some soldiers to Barnsley and I hear that some Horsemen are come to his House in Cawthorne.

Spencer-Stanhope Muniments, 60586, 11 April 1812, Sheffield City Library.

document 42

Benjamin Gott's croppers, 1803

Sixty-seven croppers went on strike to prevent an attempt by Benjamin Gott to increase the number of apprentices in case it led to lower wages.

The squabble began about some apprentices Mr Gott had taken on with the Croppers not approving, very impudently insisted should be discharged & Gott, like a man of spirit, refused to discharge them upon which all his shops were laid under an interdict & his business in a great means at a standstill—not a single Cropper would strike a stroke for him. Gott . . . finding the Croppers would weary him out at last called for help from other Merchants, some of whom . . . requested the Mayor to call a meeting. . . . Before ten o'clock in the morning of the day when the meeting was to be held, many hundreds of Croppers had assembled in the White Cloth Hall yard . . . waiting the event of our Meeting. . . . The Merchants instead of making good their complaint, directed the whole attention of the Meeting to the legality or illegality of taking apprentices & let the subject of Combination slip through entirely. . . . Mr Strother, a considerable merchant, slipped out of the Meeting during the debate & actually delivered the message the Croppers had fathered on him. . . . The Merchants, after this, formed a Committee to deal with the Croppers and when the meeting was over the Croppers gave a shout and withdrew . . . the next day the Croppers gave out they had a victory. We also heard they were in further training by a West of England Attorney none of ours being blasted enough for their purpose.

John Beckett to Earl Fitzwilliam, 28 January 1803, WWM F45/117, Sheffield City Library.

Activities of the Luddites

A summary of the damages inflicted by the rioters on various mills in the West Riding in 1811-12.

Amongst the mischief committed by or attributed to the Luddites was the burning of the gig-mill at Oatlands, near Leeds and Hawksworth corn mills, near Otley and the destruction of the machinery in the dressing shops of Joseph Hirst of Huddersfield, William Hinchliffe of Leymoor; John Garner of Honley; Clement Dyson of Dungeon, Francis Vickerman of Taylor Hill; William Thompson of Rawdon; Mr Smith of Snowgatehead near Holmfirth, James Brook of Reins and Joseph Foster of Horbury. About £500 of cloth was torn and cut into shreds in the finishing shops of Dickenson, Carr & Shann of Water Lane, Leeds and besides the destruction of their machinery, many of the above named manufacturers had their houses plundered and their furniture and windows broken to pieces. . . . Sixty-six persons were apprehended and committed to the County Gaol on various charges connected with these disturbances and in the January following a special commission of Oyer and Terminer was held at York for the purpose of trying the offenders. Eighteen of the prisoners, including three of Mr Horsfall's murderers, were capitally convicted and seventeen of them were executed on Friday 16 January 1813.

J. Mayhan, *Annals of Leeds, York and Surrounding Districts,* 1880, i. 236.

Croppers' song

One of the many songs, locally composed, which are alleged to have been sung by the Luddites on their expeditions and at their meetings.

Come Cropper lads of high renown
Who love to drink good ale that's brown,
And strike each haughty tyrant down,
With hatchet, pike and gun.

Chorus: Oh, the Cropper lads for me,
Who with lusty stroke
The shear frame broke;
The Cropper lads for me.

What though the specials still advance,
And soldiers nightly round us prance,
The Cropper lads still lead the dance,
With hatchet, pike and gun.

And night by night, when all is still
And the moon is tied behind the hill,
We forward march to do our will
With hatchet, pike and gun.

Great Enoch still shall lead the van,
Stop him who dare, stop him who can:
Press forward every gallant man,
With hatchet, pike and gun.

R. Brook, *Story of Huddersfield*, MacGibbon and Kee, 1968.

document 45

Watch and ward against rioters, 1812

Food riots also accompanied machine breaking so associations were formed to keep watch and ward for rioters.

At Barnsley there are Foot and Horse about 250 also at Penistone and other villages near. . . . Should any attempt be made to plunder the Mills, for Meal and Flower, as the Millers are now all alarmed and dare not take any up. The Thrashing Machines too seem a plea for them—many are already taken down . . . 'till things are more settled. I have desired Peter Watson to take his down and hope Mr Thorp also, he says they have watched theirs for several nights. . . . I understand they're making a fuss in protecting Bretton Hall (Wakefield) by having a number of men in the House and also have begun watch and ward in the village . . .

John Howson to John Spencer, 26 April 1812, 60564 Spencer Stanhope Muniments, Sheffield City Library.

Reports from constables on associations, 1812

The Lord Lieutenant of Yorkshire called for reports from the constables concerning associations, watch and patrolling during the time of the Luddite riots.

HUDDERSFIELD. Divided into Classes—go round the Town in 2 or 3 parties every night—an association formed—the Military attend them every night. 10 or 12 meet and patrol for a few hours.

HONLEY. The Watch go round every night—57 Special Constables sworn in—5 or 6 go round at a time—no association some arms have been stolen some time ago but at present all quiet.

ELLAND WITH GREETLAND. Patrole every night with the Military—the public houses shut up at 10 every night—the disaffected greatly exasperated—the Military force being increased to 80—the people suffering much from the price of Bread are disposed to join in any mischief.

DEWSBURY. No association—3 Watchmen every night—23 Special Constables sworn—30 more ready—if can make out 100, will form an association—the majority of persons of property refuse to come forward—no Disturbances.

Wentworth Woodhouse Muniments, WWM/F46, Sheffield City Library.

Weavers' riots in Barnsley, 1829

A severe slump in trade with reduced wages for weavers led to serious rioting for hand loom weavers felt their livelihood was in danger.

No one is without fear as to whose turn it may be next. It is said Mr Fred Wentworth sent them £20 after burning

Keresforth Hall to save the Castle. By todays post, I send you the Mercury of Saturday which brings down the riotous proceedings to Friday noon. . . . In the afternoon came Lord Wharncliffe & Dr C . . . and Ashton says he could not do anything without the consent of a general meeting of Weavers from whom they need their instructions. . . . Lord Wharncliffe, after so many years as Chairman of the Pontefract Sessions must know the law as well as Mr Justice Bailey yet in the meeting here he evidently blenched his knowledge to find fault with the Inhabitants as Special Constables. The Room at the White Bear was crowded [but] all went away dissatisfied with his Lordship. All Warehouses are now watched. . . . One of their Weaver's shops, Tees sent men to protect or when the Mob came some firing took place and a child was hurt . . .

D. Beckett to John Spencer, 15 September 1829, Spencer-Stanhope 60607, Sheffield City Library.

document 48

Disastrous fire at Colne Bridge Mills, 1818

In this cotton mill, children were employed on night work and were locked in. On this occasion the key could not be found and seventeen were burned to death within thirty minutes. This incident was raised in the Commons in connection with the Factory Act of 1819.

On Saturday morning last, a most destructive and calamitous fire broke out in the Cotton Factory of Mr Thomas Atkinson situate at Colne-Bridge, three miles from Huddersfield . . . in which the lives of seventeen female children were lost.

It appears that the Machinery . . . was worked by night as well as by day, and that about five o'clock in the morning, a boy . . . James Thornton had been sent down to the card room for rovings with a naked candle instead of the lamp. . . . One of the overlookers hastened after the lad but in vain. . . . he perceived the flames rising from a quantity of cotton and carded laps . . . Thornton . . . ran upstairs to communicate the appalling tidings that the factory was on fire. He . . . escaped from the building; but so rapid was the spread of the flames that a girl who followed him out of one of the spinning rooms dropped through the landing and perished in the flames. . . . the attention of the persons assembled was directed to rescuing the persons within who were all girls from the fate that awaited them. . . . A ladder was placed against a small window at the end of the factory but every endeavour to induce the children to approach the ladder failed. On breaking the window a dense column of smoke which soon burst into flames issued from the opening. . . . Renewed efforts were made to ascertain the place where the children might have fled . . . but in the midst of these exertions the roof and floors fell in. . . . In less than half an hour the entire building all the machinery and every article of stock was destroyed . . . Not a vestige of property was saved.

Twenty-six persons were at work in the mill; nine escaped and seventeen died; the remains of fifteen bodies were recovered but two were reduced to ashes. The ages of the dead were from nine to eighteen.

Leeds Mercury, 21 February 1818.

document 49

An attack on John Marshall during the election of 1826

Marshall was a flax spinner at Holbeck, Leeds and his treatment of child labour was notorious. He was standing as one of the candidates for the county at the election, hence this attack.

Humbly dedicated to Mr John Marshall, Flax Spinner, Holbeck.
This is the House that Jack built.
This is the Flax all heckled and torn that lay in the House that Jack built.
These are the Children all forlorn, who toil and slave from night till morn, in spinning the flax all heckled and torn, that lays in the House that Jack built.
This is the man, all shaven and shorn, for whom the children all forlorn toil and slave from night till morn, in spinning the Flax all heckled and torn, that lays in the House that Jack built.
This is John Bull, a Freeman born, whom the Man with the

head all shaven and shorn, thinks to lead by the nose, while talking of corn, while the poor Children, all forlorn, get so little for toiling from night till morn, in spinning his flax all heckled and torn, that lays in the House that Jack built.

This is the Lord (Lord Milton) so very high born, who treated his LONGWOOL friends with scorn, yet has joined the man all shaven and shorn, to lead John Bull by the nose, by talking of Corn, but if they don't mind they'll be tossed and torn, or be sent with the Children all forlorn, to twist from the Flax all heckled and torn, a Rope for to hang themselves some morn, in front of THE HOUSE THAT JACK BUILT.

Election Speeches and Squibs 1807-1830, Yorkshire Archaeological Society, 1830.

document 50

Oastler's letter to the press on Yorkshire slavery, 1830

Following his meeting with John Wood of Bradford, Richard Oastler wrote the letter to the Leeds Mercury of which the following is an extract.

Thousands of our fellow creatures and fellow subjects both male and female, the miserable inhabitants of a Yorkshire town, (Yorkshire now represented in this parliament by the giant of anti-slavery principles) are at this very moment existing in a state of slavery, more horrid that are the victims of that hellish system, 'colonial slavery'. These innocent creatures drawl out, unpitied their short but miserable existence in a place famed for its profession of religious zeal, whose inhabitants are ever foremost in professing 'temperance' and 'reformation' and are striving to out run their neighbours in missionary exertions, and would fain send the Bible to the farthest corner of the globe—aye in the very place where the anti-slavery fever rages her charity is not more admired on earth. . . . The very streets which receive the droppings of the 'Anti-Slavery Society' are wet by the tears of the innocent victims at the accursed shrine of avarice who are compelled (not by the cart whip of the negro slave driver) but by the dread of the equally appalling thong or strap of the overlooker, to haste half-dressed but not half fed, to those magazines of British infantile slavery—the worsted mills in the town and neighbourhood of Bradford. . . . Thousands of little children, both male and female, but principally female from seven to fourteen years of age, are daily compelled to labour from six o'clock in the morning to seven in the evening, with only . . . thirty minutes allowed for eating and recreation. Poor infants, you are sacrificed at the shrine of avarice . . . you are compelled to work as long as the necessity of your needy parents may require, or the cold blooded avarice of you worse than barbarian masters may demand. . . . You are doomed to labour from morning to night for one who cares not how soon your weak and tender frames are stretched to breaking.

Leeds Mercury, 30 September 1830.

document 51

Richard Webster reports on conditions in Halifax, 1830

Webster followed up the accusation by Oastler that the Bradford Mills were bad, by pointing out it was no different in Halifax.

There is not a mill in the whole town of Halifax which allows a single moment either for breakfast or tea—and the time for dinner is much the same as those in Bradford. But I believe the hours of labour to be longer than those at Bradford. None of the mills in this town stop sooner than half past seven, and some of them not before half past eight or nine o'clock and the attendance of the children is required at six in the morning. . . . Let anyone walk through the mills at the time of breakfast, and see the poor children eating their coarse fare, whilst at the same time they must attend to the respective machines at which they are employed—like beasts of burden, they must eat and work—and I am sure that an individual after seeing this if he were a Christian—if he were a man, he would blush to see the degradation to which those children were brought by the avarice of their employers. I do not, however, mean to charge this epithet upon all the manufacturers of this town, quite the reverse, I know there are honourable exceptions, but at the same time there are individuals who would not care to exact labour from them both day and night, consequently those who are possessed of more humanity are obliged, however reluctantly, to follow the same rule.

Leeds Mercury, 8 November 1830.

document 52

Halifax meeting of master spinners, 5 March 1831

The master spinners of Halifax met in the Old Cock Inn on 5 March 1831, under the chairmanship of James Ackroyd, to present arguments against reduction in hours of work.

1. The condition of those employed in the worsted mills does not warrant the conclusion that the present usages of trade are injurious to health and comfort of this class of operatives; and that the present term of labour (viz. twelve hours per day) is not attended with any consequences injurious to those employed, and is not more than adequate and necessary to provide for their livelihood.

2. An enactment which will abridge the hours of labour, or limit the age of children employed in worsted mills will produce the following effect; It will cause a proportionate reduction in wages of this class. It will materially cripple the means of those who have large young families, who in many instances are the main support of their parents. It will raise the price of goods to the consumers, which will affect the home trade considerably, and will produce the most serious effects upon the prosperity of this district, by tending to foster the manufactures of foreign nations, our trade with whom depends upon the cheap, advantageous terms on which we supply them with goods. . . . It will throw out of employment and the means of existence, of numbers of children now beneficially engaged in worsted mills and a corresponding proportion of wool-sorters, combers, weavers, and all other classes necessary to produce the present supply of goods. . . . The agriculturalists will also feel the effects of the diminished consumption of wool in no slight degree.

3. That the age to which it is proposed to limit those employed in worsted mills will be inefficient in securing the advantages which are desired, in as much as the period between fourteen and twenty-one is the most critical period in the life of those employed and that those between the ages of seven and fourteen are capable of undergoing long continued hours of labour, than those of the ages before named. . . . For confirmation of this we would appeal to all medical men of the district.

Leeds Mercury, 5 March 1831.

document 53

Address of the Manchester operatives 1833

Following the disclosure of the working conditions in cotton mills, this appeal was published in the press to forestall an attempt by mill owners to prevent any reduction in working hours.

Fellow countrymen—this sort of oppression is not confined to our own generation, or our own country. It has been attributed to the corn laws; but when this system was in its infancy no corn law existed, the hours of labour exacted from children were as bad or worse than now. It has been traced to taxation, which we feel bears heavily upon us and unequally. . . . But in America, this at all events is not the cause of over-labour in factories, and there they work children in many cases longer than they do here. In fact, it is avarice which is the root of the evil—avarice which has not been content to supplant human labour by machinery, but now asserts with bloody arrogance, its right to grind to the dust the helpless child. . . . Will you stand by and view this with cold Indifference? . . . The Ten Hours Bill is a sample in legislation favourable to us all.

Manchester Mercury, 25 April 1833.

Manchester Factory children petition for the Commission

At the conclusion of a demonstration by the factory children the following petition was presented to the Commissioners at the York Hotel.

Gentlemen, We, children employed in the factories of Manchester, beg leave to present to you this our humble and respectful memorial. We implore your pity and compassion for our sufferings, for the great weight of labour thrown on our limbs—for the long duration of that labour daily mostly in the close air of the heated room—for the weakness it brings upon us while we are little, and the sickness and deformity which fall upon many of us—for the overwhelming fatigue which numbs our senses and for the shutting out of any chance to read and write like children in other employment.

We respect our masters and are willing to work for our support, and that of our parents, and brothers, and sisters; but we want time for more rest, a little play, and to learn to read and write. Young as we are, we find that we could do our work better if we were to work less time. . . . We do not think it right that we should know nothing but work and suffering from Monday morning to Saturday night to make others rich.

P. Grant, *History of Factory Legislation*, 1866, p. 46

Handbill giving notice of arrival of Commissioners

This handbill which was posted in West Riding towns and in Lancashire expresses the discontent aroused by the inquiries of the Commissioners and shows the reception prepared for them.

APPROACH OF THE ENEMY
Copy of a Letter from an Operative at Leicester, dated 27 April 1833.

You will be surprised to hear that wee have had the head Commissioner here to-day, they had got my name and wanted me to assist them — BUT I asked them whether they was come to get EVIDENCE for the Masters, or what was their errand, for I assured them it was my opinion that they had Evidence enough already to Satisfy any Reasonable Man, and as I thought the Commission was uncalled for, I could not but protest against it, and would not recognize them in any way whatever. They spoke at length, to some of the Men in the Factory, and asked a great many Questions and told them they should want them at some Future Period. OUR MASTER TOLD THEM HE THOUGHT TEN HOURS QUITE SUFFICIENT FOR THE CHILDREN TO WORK. — I shall watch their movements while they stop here. I expect the Commission will be in Derbyshire on Monday so that our Friends must be on the look out.

Yours J. Brierley.

Leeds City Library, Miscellaneous.

document 56

Burning of the Commissioners, 1833.

Dr Thomas Chalmers visited Huddersfield in June 1833 and stayed at the George Hotel where he observed the demonstration against the Commissioners.

On entering Huddersfield, I found that in respect of fairs, I was out of the frying pan into the fire; for before my inn door, the George, there as a prodigious assemblage of people at a market; and I had to wait some time ere I could get a room for the evening. The crowd was vastly augmented by there being furthermore a political meeting in the open air, and the whole of the spacious market place was filled with the multitude. Mr Oastler held forth on the sufferings of the factory children, and was enthusiastically cheered, I saw from my window but heard not. Then followed, to me, an original scene, the burning of the Factory Commissioners and Captain Fenton, one of their obnoxious members of Parliament, and another unpopular manufacturer in effigy. The figures were fearfully like men, and being dark, the conflagration lighted up the whole square, and revealed the faces of the yelling myriads, so as to give the aspect and character of Pandemonium to the scene. The burning figures were tossed ferociously into the air and . . . were dashed into a bonfire from time to time. The spectacle . . . is a depraving one and fitted to prepare the actors for burning the originals instead of the copies.

Voice of the West Riding, 22 June 1833.

document 57

A factory inspector's problems

The report of Robert Baker, superintendent of factories, upon the over-working of boys and the reluctance of the magistrates to levy severe fines. The mill concerned was that of Taylor Ibbotson & Co of Dewsbury, Yorks.

The district where the mill of these gentlemen is situated is near Dewsbury, in Yorkshire, a neighbourhood inadequately populated, and employed entirely in the manufacture of shoddy cloths and blankets. Shoddy cloth is made from woollen rags torn in pieces by a powerful machine, reduced as far as possible to their original form of wool, mixed with flocks and worked up again into cloth . . .

In tearing up of these rags a great quantity of dust is produced so that . . . persons standing three yards apart cannot clearly distinguish each other. The rooms are excessively small and the machines require great power to drive them . . . and the engines are unable to turn the machinery for the day with the shoddy machines added to it. These shoddy machines had . . . in four mills been worked in the night, after other machinery had ceased.

The boys . . . stated they commenced work on Friday 27 May last at six a.m. and with the exception of meal hours and one hour at midnight extra they did not cease working till four o'clock on Saturday evening having been two days and a night thus engaged.

I . . . varied the information so as to enable me to sue for £80 being four full penalties for working two boys more than twelve hours, a boy before 5 a.m. on the Saturday and for working two boys in the night time. . . . These views were not responded to by the magistrate before whom the case was heard. The parties were fined only £5 on each information and with an aggregate of penalties of £20 escaped.

The defendants pleaded guilty . . . and that this was their first offence. It is more probable . . . that this was the first offence of Taylor & Co. but from night-working having been practised by other persons more than once in the same neighbourhood . . . I have reason to believe that had not these parties been discovered and punished such practices would have continued.

Robert Baker to Lord John Russell, 14 June 1836.
C.R. Wing, *Evils of the Factory System,* London 1837, xxiii.

document 58

An attack by plug rioters, 1842

Joseph Cooper of Holehouse Mill, Glossop, was attacked by rioters on his way home from court on the grounds that he was prosecuting the strikers.

On my return home from the court held at the Silk Mill yesterday, Myself and Two sons with James Cooper of Hill-Top and John Howard of Holehouse agreed to make our way home without making any stay at Glossop and set off intending to turn to our left at the Beehive and go over the Weir above Shepley Mill and through the wood home. But we were recognised opposite the Beehive by two women who said we were the prosecutors and instigated the Mob against us and they instantly began to throw stones, at us, we could not go back and the only way left for us was to flee for our lives which we did and John Howard took refuge in the house of Samuel Robinson of the free Town and the rest of us ran towards Bridgefield. Three of us took refuge in the house of Mr Joseph Howard but my son Joseph kept forward and was overtaken by the Mob who struck him on the head with a stone and beat him and returned to the house of Mr Howard and surrounded it till we were relieved by the Constables; my

Son is not able to get out of bed. One of the instigators is known to us, if not both. Look to Joseph Lawton's Bail for his mother was the principal alluded to.

Joseph Cooper to Michael Ellison of Glossop Hall, 30 August 1842, Arundel Castle Muniments, ACM/D324, Sheffield City Library.

document 59

Strikers' handbill, 1844

During a strike those weavers in employment were expected to assist those suffering from loss of earnings. Those who refused were warned.

TAKE NOTICE: there are nine weavers at Spring Mill Works at Royton, employed by Saville & Co who have left their work in consequence of not being fairly remunerated for their labour. We have been receiving 7d per cut of 29 yards in length, 28 inches width, 14 picks per ¼ inch. The Standard price in Royton is 9½d and 10d per cut for the same amount of work. This is the third week of the strike and we sincerely hope the calico weavers of the borough will come forward with their cordial support. We can assure you, we are reduced to the utmost distress, having only worked a fortnight since the establishment commenced and some of us were unemployed for many weeks before. 'Withold not good from them to whom it is due, when it is in the power of thine hand to do it 'Proverbs iii, v.27.

The Committee would be glad to see a very strong meeting of weavers on Wednesday in the Chartists Room, Oldham.

At Walshaw Mill, there is Elizabeth Neild and Sarah Neild and a few others that will be exposed if they do not pay. At Greenbank Mill, Bill Brierly has two shares in the Henpecked Club and his wife will not let him pay.

£20.15s.9½d was raised and seventy-six weavers received 5s.1d each.

J. Boardman, *Cotton Spinning in Oldham*, York 1971.

Report on two contrasting mills

There were wide variations in the standard of ventilation, cleanliness, lighting and amenities in Lancashire mills. The one at Egerton is far ahead of the Oldham mill in every respect.

Ashworth's mills lie . . . in Egerton at the bottom of a deep wooded valley. The mills . . . are propelled by steam and water power, and a huge wheel for the latter purpose, sixty feet in diameter, is really one of the sights of Lancashire. The number of hours worked at this establishment is eleven a day, and the time of labour commences at six o'clock. . . . The general arrangements of cotton mills are very similar but I can confidently speak of the excellent arrangements of Ashworth's establishment. The large card, roving and drawing room in the basement story is fully eleven feet from floor to ceiling and perfectly ventilated. . . . The windows are very large and provided with full arrangements for swinging panes. . . . I afterwards went over two small mills in Oldham. . . . Both were dirty and constructed in the old-fashioned unventilated style. The workpeople looked more gaunt, yellow and slatterly than they are in the average of factories; but I saw nothing calling for any special notice, over and above what I have said of the coarse spinning mill . . . where the stairs were rickety and filth encrusted and the drawing and spinning room not only hot, but what is much worse, choking and stifling and reeking with oil

A.B. Reach, *Manchester and the Textile District,* 1849.

New machines at Farnworth, 1860

George Horrocks, assuming that prosperity unlimited lay ahead, installed new throstle frames in his mill and he describes how they started up the first machine.

I started my first Throstle on Saturday Dec. 1st driven by a new 2½in diam pollished shaft; large pullies, bored and trued, with Conical Keys to fit the Shaft all made true and balanced, the whole of the scheming of each plan, and the calculating of the size, and exact place of each pulley with swing pullies, is entirely my own. . . . I went up the ladder and seized the strap with my lame hand and gave it one sweep and on it went, and ran exactly right both upon the main pulley & swing pulleys. . . . I received great praise from all who looks at it particularly Dobsons men who are fitting the throstles up, the spindles run about 5,000 revolutions per minute and will clear to me about five pounds £5.0.0 per week, thank God.

Letter from George Horrocks of Farnworth to his son William, Horrocks Papers, DP412/58, Lancashire Record Office.

document 62

Industrial problems 1863

This letter from George Horrocks to his son William reveals the problems facing manufacturers as the result of the American Civil War. 13 May.

Our mind is a little troubled on account of the American war; getting Cotton to such a high price, and what makes it worse we cannot see the end; we trust the Lord our God will guide us safe and right. . . . The Whitsuntide holidays are drawing near and the news paper recommends all parties to stop a full week and then run short time what will be done I cannot tell yet. I shall stop my Looms about 4 or 5 days and by then I pray the Lord may improve our position. . . . The Ranters new Chapel in queen Street Farnworth was opened yesterday and your Brother Henry attended as *usual* on such occasions. . . . Samuel Hardman . . . got his new mill to work about the time you was at home last. He has been selling his yarns to a man who has failed in about £30,000 and S Hardman is in £4,000 it has allmost undone his mind. . . . T Nuttal & Son began to build a new mill some time since but they have stopped building for the present until there is something better. Wm Openshaw & Co have got some machinery to work but Wm has a very long face. Wallwork & Sussins Mill is stopped yet or else just beginning again . . .

Letter George Horrocks to William, 13 May 1963, DP412/83, Lancashire Record Office.

document 63

Problems facing the cotton worker, 1864

The diary of John Ward highlights the conditions facing the operatives during the Civil War.

10 April. It has been a poor time for me all the time owing to the American war, which seems as far of being settled as ever. The mill I work in was stopped all last winter during which time I had three shillings per week allowed by the relief committee which barely kept me alive. When we started work again it was with Surat cotton, and a great number of weavers can only mind two looms. We can earn very little. I have not earned a shilling a day this last month and there are many like me. . . . The principal reason why I did not write any notes this last two years is because I was sad and weary. One half the time I was out of work, the other I had to work as hard as ever I wrought in my life and can hardly keep myself living . . . I can't go much further with what I am at.

Diary of John Ward 1860-4, *Historic Society of Lancashire and Cheshire*, vol. cv.

Bibliography

PRIMARY

Articles Preparatory to Visitation, EDV7/1/83, Cheshire Record Office
Proctors' Trade Papers, Borthwick Institute of Historical Research, York
Cornelius Ashworth's Diary 1782-1784, Halifax Central Library
John Firth's Letter Book 1739, HAS321, Halifax Central Library
Porteus Diaries 1777-1809, Lambeth Palace Library
Kirkham Parish Records, PR827/168, Lancashire Record Office
Bishops' Register Transcripts, Lancashire Record Office
Scarisbrick Papers, DDSC12/135, Lancashire Record Office
Thomas Marsden's Festing Accounts, Lancashire Record Office
Lancashire Wills, Lancashire Record Office
Eccleston Papers DDSc.12, Lancashire Record Office
Lancashire Evening Post 1777, DP, Lancashire Record Office
Quarter Sessions Orders, 1779, 1780, 1781, 1784, Lancashire Record Office
Quarter Sessions Petitions, 1813, Lancashire Record Office
Horrocks of Farnworth, DP412/58/83, Lancashire Record Office
Kenyon MSS, Historial Manuscripts Commission
Earl of Dartmouth Rentals, Leeds City Archives
Kirkgate Wills 1684, DB147/1, Leeds City Archives
Sutcliffe Papers 133, 143, Leeds City Archives
State Papers Domestic (Petitions) 254, Public Record Office
Marquis of Crewe Muniments, CM 969,970, Sheffield Central Library
Spencer Stanhope Muniments, 60586,60564,60607, Sheffield Central Library
Wentworth Woodhouse Muniments, F.45/117,F.46, Sheffield Central Library
Arundel Castle Muniments, ACM/D324

PRIMARY PRINTED

1 *Commons Journals*, Report on Petitions of Master and Journeymen Weavers 1800, vols. xx–xlix
2 Defoe, D., *Journal of a Tour through England and Wales*, London, 1738.

3   *Election Speeches and Squibs 1807-1830*, Leeds, 1831.
4   *Factory Inquiry Commission 1st Report*, Section D, 1833, London, 1834.
5   France, R. Sharpe, 'Diary of John Ward, weaver, of Clitheroe', *Lancashire and Cheshire Historic Society*, vol. cv.
6   Farrer, K.E., *Correspondence of Josiah Wedgwood 1781-94*, London, 1906.
7   *Leeds Intelligencer*, 1793, 1804.
8   *Leeds Mercury*, 1790, 1818, 1830, 1831, 1833.
9   *Manchester Courier* 1846.
10 *Manchester Mercury*, 1809, 1833.
11 Porteus, B. *Letter to the Clergy of Chester concerning Sunday Schools*, London, 1786.
12 *Report of the Visitors to the Cotton Mills 1807*, London, 1808.
13 Tawney, R.H. and Power, E., eds, Tudor Economic Documents, vols. i-iii, Longmans, 1951.
14 *Report on the Woollen Industry 1806*, London, 1807.
15 *Voice of the West Riding 1833*, Leeds, 1833.
16 Yorkshire Archaeological Society, *Lay Subsidy Rolls, Record Series* xvi.
17 Yorkshire Archaeological Society, *Wakefield Manor Court Rolls, Record Series* i-iv.
18 Young, A., *A Six Months Tour through the North of England*, London, 1770.

GENERAL
19 Addy, J., *The Agrarian Revolution*, Longman, 1972.
20 Addy, J., *Denby Dale Urban District Council: a short history*, Huddersfield, 1974
21 Addy, J., *'Two eighteenth century Bishops of Chester'*, unpublished Ph.D. thesis, Leeds, 1972.
22 Aikin, J., *Description of the Country 30 to 40 miles around Manchester*, London, 1798.
23 Alfred, S.K., *History of the Factory Movement*, vol. i, London, 1857.
24 Arnold, R.A., *History of the Cotton Famine*, London, 1864.
25 Ashmore, O., *James Garnet of Clitheroe*, Historic Society of Lancashire and Cheshire, vols. 121,123.
26 Ashton, J., *Manchester Guide, 1804*, Manchester, 1804.
27 Ashton, T.S., *The Industrial Revolution 1760-1830*, Oxford U.P., 1868.
28 Ashton, T.S., *'The standard of life of the workers in England'*, *Economic History Review*, 1949.

29   Aspin, C. and Chapman, S.D., *James Hargreaves and the Spinning Jenny*, Helmshore Local History Society, 1964.

30   Axon, W.E.A., *Annals of Manchester*, Manchester, 1886.

31   Baines, E., *History of Cotton Manufacture in Great Britain*, London, 1835.

32   Bamford, S., *Dialect of South Lancashire*, London, 1850.

33   Barlow, A., *History and Principles of Weaving*, London, 1878.

34   Bentley, P., *Inheritance*, London, Gollancz, 1932.

35   Bird, A., *Roads and Vehicles*, Longman, 1973.

36   Bowden, W., *Industrial Society in England*, New York, 1925.

37   Boyson, R., *The Ashworth Cotton Enterprise*, Oxford U.P., 1970.

38   Briggs, A., *The Age of Improvement*, Longmans, 1959.

39   Briggs, A., *Chartist Studies*, Macmillan, 1963.

40   Brontë, C., *Shirley*, London, 1849.

41   Butt, J.M., *Robert Owen, Prince of Cotton Spinners* David & Charles, 1971.

42   Butterworth, E., *History of Oldham*, Oldham, 1833.

43   Butterworth, J., *History of the Trade of Manchester*, Manchester, 1962.

44   Bythell, D., *The Handloom Weavers*, Cambridge U.P., 1969.

45   Carter, T., *Memoirs of a Working Man*, London, 1845.

46   Chadwick, D., *The Rate of Wages 1839-1859*, London, 1860.

47   Chaloner, W.H., *People and Industries*, Cass, 1963.

48   Chaloner, W.H., 'Robert Owen, Peter Drinkwater and the early factory system in Manchester', *Bulletin of John Rylands Library*, xxxvii.

49   Chapman, D.S., *The Early Factory Masters*, David & Charles, 1967.

50   Chapman, S.D., 'The Peels in the early cotton industry', *Business History*, xi (1969).

51   Chapman, S.D., *The Cotton Industry in the Industrial Revolution*, London, Macmillan, 1972.

52   Chapman, S.D., 'Pioneers of worsted spinning by power', *Business History*, vii.

53   Chapman, S.J., *Lancashire Cotton Industry*, Manchester, 1904.

54   Clarke, C.A., *The Effects of the Factory System*, 1965.

55   Cole, G.D.H., *History of Socialist Thought*, vol. i, Macmillan, 1953.

56   Collier, F., 'Family economy and the working classes in the cotton industry', *Chetham Society Publications*, third series vol. xii.

57   Cooke-Taylor, W., *Modern Factory System*, London, 1895.

58   Cooke-Taylor, W., *Notes of a Tour in the Manufacturing Districts of Lancashire*, London, 1844.

59 Croft, W.R., *Oastler and His Times,* Huddersfield, 1881.

60 Crump, W.B., 'Leeds woollen industry', *Thoresby Society,* Leeds, 1931, vol. xxxii.

61 Crump, W.B. and Ghorbals, G., *Huddersfield Woollen and Worsted Industry*, Huddersfield, 1935.

62 Daniels, G.W., *Early English Cotton Industry*, Manchester, 1970.

63 Darvall, F.O., *Population Disturbances in Regency England*, Oxford U.P., 1954, (repr. 1970).

64 Davies, R.E., *Life of Robert Owen*, London, 1907.

65 Dobson, R.P., *The Evolution of the Spinning Machine*, Manchester, 1910.

66 Driver, C., *Tory Radical: the life of Richard Oastler*, Oxford U.P., New York, 1946.

67 Dyer, J., *The Fleece* III, London 1770.

68 Eden, F.M., *The State of the Poor (1797)*, ed. A.G.L. Rogers, Routledge, 1928.

69 Edwards, M.M., *The British Cotton Trade 1780-1815*, Manchester, 1967.

70 English, W., *The Textile Industry*, Longmans, 1969.

71 Fairbairn, W., *Mills and Millwork*, London, 1863.

72 Ferriar, J., *Proceedings of the Board of Health, Manchester*, London, 1805.

73 Fitton, R.S. and Wadsworth, A.P., *The Strutts and the Arkwrights*, 2nd ed., Manchester U.P., 1973.

74 French, C.J., *Life and Times of Samuel Crompton*, London, 1859.

75 Fryde, E.B., *Wool Accounts of William de la Pole*, York, St Anthony's Press, 1964.

76 Fryde, E.B., *Some Business Transactions of York Merchants*, York, St Anthony's Press, 1966.

77 *Gentleman's Magazine*, lxxii, (1802).

78 George, D.M., 'Some causes of the increase of population in the eighteenth century', *Economic Journal*, xx, xii.

79 Gill, J.C., *The Ten Hours Parson*, SPCK, 1959.

80 Grant, P., *History of the Ten Hours Bill*, Manchester, 1866.

81 Gregg, P., *Social and Economic History of England*, London, Harrap, 1965.

82 Guest, R., *Compendious History of Cotton Manufacture*, Manchester, 1823.

83 Hadfield, C. and Biddle, G., *Canals of North West England*, David & Charles, 1970.

84 Hammond, J. and Hammond, B., *The Bleak Age*, London 1934.

85   Hammond, J. and Hammond, B., *The Rise of Modern Industry*, London 1937.

86   Hammond, J. and Hammond, B., *The Skilled Labourer*, London 1927.

87   Hammond, J. and Hammond, B., *The Town Labourer*, London 1941.

88   Heaton, H., 'Benjamin Gott and the Industrial Revolution in Yorkshire', *Economic History Review*, iii.

89   Heaton, H., *The Yorkshire Woollen and Worsted Industry*, Oxford 1929.

90   Henderson, W.O., *The Lancashire Cotton Famine*, Manchester 1934.

91   Hill, C.P., *British Social and Economic History*, London, E. Arnold, 1970.

92   Hills, R.L., *Power in the Industrial Revolution*, Manchester 1960.

93   Hirst, W., *History of the Woollen Trade for the last sixty Years*, Leeds, 1844.

94   Hopwood, E., *The Lancashire Weavers' Story*, Manchester 1969.

95   Hutchins, B.L., and Harrison, A., *History of Factory Legislation*, London, 1903.

96   James, J., *History of Bradford*, Bradford, 1841.

97   James, J., *History of Worsted Manufacture*, London, 1857.

98   Jones, J., *The Cotton Mill*, Manchester, 1821.

99   Kaye, J.P., *Moral and Physical Conditions of the Working Class in the Cotton Manufacture of Manchester*, London, 1832.

100 Kennedy, J., 'A brief memoir of Samuel Crompton', *Manchester Literary and Philosophical Society*, vol. v (1831).

101 Lipson, E., *History of the Woollen and Worsted Industry*, London, 1855.

102 Lord, J., *Capital and Steam Power 1760-1800*, London, 1923.

103 Lord, W., *Memoir of John Kay*, Rochdale, 1903.

104 McConnell & Co., *A Century of Fine Cotton Spinning*, Manchester, 1913.

105 McCord, N., *The Anti-Corn Law League*, London, Allen & Unwin, 1968.

106 McCreedy, H.W., 'Elizabeth Gaskell and the Cotton Famine in Lancashire', *Historic Society of Lancashire and Cheshire*, vol. 123.

107 Mantoux, P., *The Industrial Revolution in the Eighteenth Century*, London 1961.

108 Marx, K., *Capital*, London, 1907.

109 Morehouse, J., *History of Kirkburton*, Huddersfield, 1861.

110 Musson, A.E. and Robinson, E., *Science and Technology in the Industrial Revolution*, Manchester, U.P., 1969.

111 Owen, R., *Life of Robert Owen*, London, 1907.

112 Peel, F., *Risings of Luddites, Chartists and Plugdrawers,* Heckmondwike, 1888.

113 Pinchbeck, I., *Early Factory Legislation,* London 1930.

114 Platt, C.P.S., *The Monastic Grange in Medieval England*, London, Macmillan, 1969.

115 Power, E., *The Medieval English Wool Trade*, London, Macmillan, 1955.

116 Purvis, J.S., *The Admiralty Court of York*, York, St Anthony's Press, 1962.

117 Ramsbotham, D., *Thoughts on the use of Machines in Cotton Manufacture*, London, 1780.

118 Rimmer, W.G., *Marshalls of Leeds, Flax Spinners 1780-1886*, Cambridge U.P., 1960.

119 Rodgers, H.B., 'The Lancashire Cotton Industry in 1840', *Transactions of the Institute of British Geographers* xxviii (1960).

120 Rogers, T., *History of Prices*, vols i-vii, London 1866-1902.

121 Rolt, L.T.C., *Navigable Waterways*, London, Longmans, 1969.

122 Rose, A.G., 'Early cotton riots in Lancashire 1769-1779', *Historic Society of Lancashire and Cheshire*, vols. 73, 74.

123 Royston-Pike, E., *Human Documents of the Industrial Revolution*, London, Allen & Unwin, 1966.

124 Sanderson, M., 'Education and Factory in Industrial Lancashire', *Economic History Review 2nd Series*, xx.

125 Sigsworth, E., *Black Dyke Mills*, Liverpool U.P., 1958.

126 Silver, A.N., *Manchester Men and Indian Cotton 1847-1972*, Manchester U.P., 1966.

127 Soloway, R.A., *Prelates and People 1780-1850*, London, Routledge, 1969.

128 Spufford, M., *Contrasting Communities*, Cambridge U.P., 1974.

129 Strank, C.J., *Dean Hook*, London 1954.

130 Sykes, D.E.F., *Huddersfield and its Vicinity*, Huddersfield, 1898.

131 Tann, J., *The Development of the Factory,* London, Cornmarket Press, 1970.

132 Taylor, W.R., *Factory System and Factory Acts*, London, 1912.

133 Thomis, M., *The Luddites*, David & Charles 1970.

134 Thompson, E.P., *Making of the English Working Class*, London 1963.

135 Tremlow, J.A. and Walker, A., *Liverpool Town Book*, I., Liverpool, 1918.

136 Trevelyan, G.M., *Social History of England*, Longmans, 1942.
137 Unwin, G., *Samuel Oldknow and the Arkwrights*, Manchester, 1924.
138 Unwin, G., 'Transition to the factory System', *English Historical Review*, xxxvi.
139 Ure, A., *Cotton Manufacture in Great Britain*, London, 1861.
140 Wadsworth, A.P. and Mann, J.L., *The Cotton Trade and Industrial Lancashire 1680-1780*, Manchester 1931.
141 Walker, J., *British Economic and Social History*, London, Macdonald & Evans, 1968.
142 Walker, R.B., 'Religious changes in Cheshire 1750-1850', *Journal of Ecclesiastical History*, April 1966.
143 Ward, J.T., *The Factory Movement*, Macmillan 1962.
144 Ward, J.T., 'Leeds and factory reform', *Thoresby Society xlvi* (1960).
145 Ward, J.T., 'Matthew Balme, factory reformer, 1813-1854', *Bradford Antiquarian viii*, 1960.
146 Watts, D.G., 'Water power and the Industrial Revolution', *Transactions of the Cumberland and Westmorland Archaeological Society*, new series lxvii.
147 Waugh, E., *Lancashire Folk in the Cotton Famine*, London, 1867.
148 Webb, S. and Webb, B., *History of Trades Unionism*, rev. ed., Longmans 1928, reissued 1950.
149 Wing, C., *Evils of the Factory System*, London, 1857.
150 Wyatt, C., 'Origins of spinning cotton by machines', *Report on Manufacture and Agriculture*, xxxii, (1818).

Index